THE WINTER'S TALE

The scene: now in Sicilia, now in Bohemia

CHARACTERS IN THE PLAY

LEONTES, *King of Sicilia*

MAMILLIUS, *young Prince of Sicilia*

CAMILLO ⎱
ANTIGONUS ⎰ *four Lords of Sicilia*
CLEOMENES
DION

POLIXENES, *King of Bohemia*

FLORIZEL, *Prince of Bohemia*

ARCHIDAMUS, *a Lord of Bohemia*

OLD SHEPHERD, *reputed father of Perdita*

CLOWN, *his son*

AUTOLYCUS, *a rogue*

A Mariner

A Gaoler

HERMIONE, *Queen to Leontes*

PERDITA, *daughter to Leontes and Hermione*

PAULINA, *wife to Antigonus*

EMILIA, *a Lady*

MOPSA ⎱
DORCAS ⎰ *shepherdesses*

Other Lords and Gentlemen, Ladies, Officers and Servants, Shepherds and Shepherdesses

TIME, *as Chorus*

THE
WINTER'S TALE

William Shakespeare

WORDSWORTH CLASSICS

The paper in this book is produced from pure wood
pulp, without the use of chlorine or any other substance
harmful to the environment. The energy used in its
production consists almost entirely of hydroelectricity
and heat generated from waste materials, thereby
conserving fossil fuels and contributing little to the
greenhouse effect.

This edition published 1995 by
Wordsworth Editions Limited
Cumberland House, Crib Street, Ware,
Hertfordshire SG12 9ET

ISBN 1 85326 235 8

Printed and bound in Denmark by Nørhaven
Typeset in the UK by The R & B Partnership

INTRODUCTION

The Winter's Tale was first performed c. 1611 and published in the First Folio of 1623. The main source is Robert Greene's romance, *Pandosto* (1588).

The first part of *The Winter's Tale* forms a rounded tragedy of jealousy. Leontes, King of Sicilia, has entertained his childhood friend, Polixenes, now King of Bohemia, for several months. Driven to a sudden and insane jealousy by the closeness of the friendship between his queen Hermione and Polixenes, he instructs his close adviser Camillo to poison Polixenes. Instead, Camillo warns Polixenes and escapes with him to Bohemia. Leontes claps his pregnant wife into prison and brings her to trial on a charge of adultery and a trumped-up accusation of conspiracy to poison him. When the Delphic oracle pronounces Hermione chaste and Leontes a 'jealous tyrant', he defies its message. His new-born daughter has already been carried off by Antigonus, unwillingly bound to expose the infant to the elements. Now comes news of the death of Leontes's son and the report from Antigonus's forceful and outraged wife Paulina that Hermione has also died. The shamed Leontes vows to spend the rest of his life in daily penance. Meanwhile Antigonus has brought the innocent daughter to the Bohemian shore, where he leaves her with a store of gold and a 'character', naming her Perdita. He is eaten by a bear while an old shepherd finds Perdita.

There follows a gap of 16 years, explained by Time as Chorus, and the second part, destined to be a comedy of rebirth and renewal, begins. Perdita, though brought up in the shepherd's humble home, has attracted the love of Polixenes's son, Prince Florizel. But Polixenes comes in disguise to attend the sheep-shearing feast and shatters the joy of the event by disclosing himself and demanding the end of the match. With Camillo's help, Perdita and Florizel escape and sail to Sicilia, where they are welcomed by Leontes. The vengeful Polixenes, who has followed them, learns, as they all do, the secret of Perdita's birth and welcomes the forthcoming marriage as a guarantee of his reconciliation with Leontes. Paulina gathers all the leading characters to see the statue of Hermione, newly completed. As Leontes looks at it with wonder, Paulina calls for music and the statue comes to life. Hermione is 'reborn' into her marriage with Leontes.

The Winter's Tale belongs with Shakespeare's other last plays *Pericles, Cymbeline* and *The Tempest*. It is a multi-faceted romance, written for indoor performance at the Blackfriars, where the stylish work of John Fletcher was much favoured. The second half focuses on the reconciliation that can be achieved through grace, a word which is allowed its full range from spiiritual to physical reference.

This Introduction is taken from *The Wordsworth Companion to Literature in English*.

Details of William Shakespeare's early life are scanty. He was the son of a prosperous merchant of Stratford upon Avon, and tradition has it that he was born on 23rd April 1564; records show that he was baptized three days later. It is likely that he attended the local Grammar School, but he had no university education. Of his early career there is no record, though John Aubrey states that he was a country schoolmaster. How he became involved with the stage is equally uncertain, but he was sufficiently established as a playwright by 1592 to be criticized in print. He was a leading member of the Lord Chamberlain's Company, which became the King's Men on the accession of James I in 1603. Shakespeare married Anne Hathaway in 1582, by whom he had two daughters and a son, Hamnet, who died in 1586. Towards the end of his life he loosened his ties with London, and retired to New Place, his substantial property in Stratford which he had bought in 1597. He died on 23rd April 1616 aged 52, and is buried in Holy Trinity Church, Stratford.

Further reading:
C L Barber: *Shakespeare's Festive Comedy*
R Berman: *A Reader's Guide to Shakespeare's Plays* 1973
S L Bethell: *The Winter's Tale* 1949
R A Foakes: Shakespeare: *The Dark Comedies to the Last Plays* 1971
F Pyle: The Winter's Tale: *A Commentary on the Structure* 1969
W Sanders: *The Winter's Tale* 1987

THE WINTER'S TALE

[1. 1.] *Sicilia. A long gallery in the palace of Leontes,
with doors at either end; chairs, tables, etc.*

'*Enter* CAMILLO *and* ARCHIDAMUS'

Archidamus. If you shall chance, Camillo, to visit Bohemia, on the like occasion whereon my services are now
on foot, you shall see, as I have said, great difference betwixt our Bohemia and your Sicilia.

Camillo. I think, this coming summer, the King of
Sicilia means to pay Bohemia the visitation which he justly
owes him.

Archidamus. Wherein our entertainment shall shame
us: we will be justified in our loves: for, indeed...

Camillo. Beseech you...   10

Archidamus. Verily I speak it in the freedom of my
knowledge: we cannot with such magnificence...in so
rare...I know not what to say...We will give you sleepy
drinks, that your senses (unintelligent of our insufficience)
may, though they cannot praise us, as little accuse us.

Camillo. You pay a great deal too dear for what's given
freely.

Archidamus. Believe me, I speak as my understanding
instructs me, and as mine honesty puts it to utterance.

Camillo. Sicilia cannot show himself over-kind to Bo-   20
hemia...They were trained together in their childhoods;
and there rooted betwixt them then such an affection,
which cannot choose but branch now. Since their more
mature dignities and royal necessities made separation of
their society, their encounters (though not personal) have
been royally attorneyed with interchange of gifts, letters,

loving embassies—that they have seemed to be together, though absent; shook hands, as over a vast; and embraced as it were from the ends of opposed winds. The heavens
30 continue their loves.

Archidamus. I think there is not in the world, either malice or matter, to alter it....You have an unspeakable comfort of your young prince Mamillius: it is a gentleman of the greatest promise that ever came into my note.

Camillo. I very well agree with you in the hopes of him: it is a gallant child; one that, indeed, physics the subject, makes old hearts fresh: they that went on crutches ere he was born desire yet their life to see him a man.

Archidamus. Would they else be content to die?
40 *Camillo.* Yes; if there were no other excuse why they should desire to live.

Archidamus. If the king had no son, they would desire to live on crutches till he had one. [*they pass out of hearing*

[I. 2.] '*Enter* LEONTES, HERMIONE, MAMILLIUS, POLIXENES,' *and attendants; Leontes, Hermione and Polixenes sit, Mamillius plays with toys*

Polixenes. Nine changes of the wat'ry star hath been
The shepherd's note, since we have left our throne
Without a burthen: time as long again
Would be filled up, my brother, with our thanks,
And yet we should, for perpetuity,
Go hence in debt: and therefore, like a cipher
(Yet standing in rich place), I multiply,
With one 'We thank you,' many thousands moe
That go before it.
    Leontes.   Stay your thanks a while,
10 And pay them when you part.
    Polixenes.   Sir, that's to-morrow...
I am questioned by my fears, of what may chance

Or breed upon our absence, that may blow
No sneaping winds at home, to make us say
'This is put forth too truly'...Besides, I have stayed
To tire your royalty.

Leontes. We are tougher, brother,
Than you can put us to't.

Polixenes. No longer stay.

Leontes. One se'nnight longer.

Polixenes. Very sooth, to-morrow.

Leontes. We'll part the time between's then: and in that
I'll no gainsaying.

Polixenes. Press me not, beseech you, so:
There is no tongue that moves...none, none i'th' world, 20
So soon as yours, could win me: so it should now,
Were there necessity in your request, although
'Twere needful I denied it. My affairs
Do even drag me homeward: which to hinder
Were (in your love) a whip to me; my stay,
To you a charge and trouble: to save both,
Farewell, our brother.

Leontes. Tongue-tied, our queen? speak you.

Hermione. I had thought, sir, to have held my peace,
until
You had drawn oaths from him not to stay: you, sir,
Charge him too coldly. Tell him, you are sure   30
All in Bohemia's well: this satisfaction
The by-gone day proclaimed—say this to him,
He's beat from his best ward.

Leontes. Well said, Hermione.

Hermione. To tell, he longs to see his son, were strong:
But let him say so then, and let him go;
But let him swear so, and he shall not stay,
We'll thwack him hence with distaffs....
[*to Polixenes*] Yet of your royal presence I'll adventure

The borrow of a week. When at Bohemia
40 You take my lord, I'll give him my commission
To let him there a month behind the gest
Prefixed for's parting: yet, good deed, Leontes,
I love thee not a jar o'th' clock behind
What Lady She her lord....You'll stay?

> [*Leontes rises and draws apart, observing*
> *Hermione and Polixenes unobserved*

Polixenes.   No, madam.
Hermione. Nay, but you will?
Polixenes.   I may not, verily.
Hermione. 'Verily!'
You put me off with limber vows: but I,
Though you would seek t'unsphere the stars with oaths,
Should yet say, 'Sir, no going'...Verily
50 You shall not go; a lady's Verily 'is
As potent as a lord's. Will you go yet?
Force me to keep you as a prisoner,
Not like a guest; so you shall pay your fees
When you depart, and save your thanks. How say you?
My prisoner? or my guest? by your dread Verily,
One of them you shall be.
  Polixenes.   Your guest then, madam:
To be your prisoner should import offending;
Which is for me less easy to commit
Than you to punish.
  Hermione.   Not your gaoler then,
60 But your kind hostess....Come, I'll question you
Of my lord's tricks and yours, when you were boys:
You were pretty lordings then?
  Polixenes.   We were, fair queen,
Two lads, that thought there was no more behind,
But such a day to-morrow, as to-day,
And to be boy eternal.

Hermione.　　　　　　　　　　Was not my lord
The verier wag o'th' two?

Polixenes.　We were as twinned lambs, that did frisk
　　　i'th' sun,
And bleat the one at th'other: what we changed
Was innocence for innocence; we knew not
The doctrine of ill-doing, nor dreamed
That any did...Had we pursued that life,　　　　　　70
And our weak spirits ne'er been higher reared
With stronger blood, we should have answered heaven
Boldly 'not guilty'; the imposition cleared,
Hereditary ours.

Hermione.　　　　By this we gather
You have tripped since.

Polixenes.　　　　　　　O my most sacred lady,
Temptations have since then been born to's: for
In those unfledged days was my wife a girl;
Your precious self had then not crossed the eyes
Of my young play-fellow.

Hermione.　　　　　　　Grace to boot!　　　　　80
Of this make no conclusion, lest you say
Your queen and I are devils: yet, go on,
　　　[*Leontes comes softly forward from behind, unseen*
Th'offences we have made you do we'll answer,
If you first sinned with us; and that with us
You did continue fault; and that you slipped not
With any, but with us.

Leontes.　　　　　　Is he won yet?

Hermione [*turns*]. He'll stay, my lord.

(*Leontes.*　　　　　　At my request he would not...
[*aloud*] Hermione, my dearest, thou never spok'st
To better purpose.

Hermione.　　　Never?

Leontes.　　　　　　　　Never, but once.

90 *Hermione*. What? have I twice said well? when was't
           before?
I prithee tell me: cram's with praise, and make's
As fat as tame things: one good deed, dying tongueless,
Slaughters a thousand waiting upon that.
Our praises are our wages: you may ride's
With one soft kiss a thousand furlongs ere
With spur we heat an acre. But to th' goal:
My last good deed was to entreat his stay;
What was my first? it has an elder sister,
Or I mistake you: O, would her name were Grace!
100 But once before I spoke to th' purpose? When?
Nay, let me have't: I long.
        Leontes.   Why, that was when
Three crabbéd months had soured themselves to death,
Ere I could make thee open thy white hand,
And clap thyself my love; then didst thou utter
'I am yours for ever.'
        Hermione.   'Tis Grace, indeed....
Why, lo you now, I have spoke to th' purpose twice:
The one, for ever earned a royal husband;
Th'other, for some while a friend.
                    [*she gives her hand to Polixenes; they
                        rise and talk apart*
(*Leontes* [*sits, watching them*].   Too hot, too hot:
To mingle friendship far, is mingling bloods.
110 I have tremor cordis on me: my heart dances,
But not for joy; not joy....This entertainment
May a free face put on; derive a liberty
From heartiness, from bounty, fertile bosom,
And well become the agent: 't may; I grant:
But to be paddling palms and pinching fingers,
As now they are, and making practised smiles
As in a looking-glass; and then to sigh, as 'twere

The mort o'th' deer; O, that is entertainment
My bosom likes not, nor my brows....Mamillius,
Art thou my boy?
 Mamillius [*looks up from play*]. Ay, my good lord.
  Leontes.   I'fecks! 120
Why, that's my bawcock....What! hast smutched thy
   nose?
They say it is a copy out of mine....[*he wipes the boy's face*]
   Come, captain,
We must be neat; not neat, but cleanly, captain:
And yet the steer, the heifer, and the calf,
Are all called 'neat'....Still virginalling
Upon his palm....How now, you wanton calf?
Art thou my calf?
 Mamillius.   Yes, if you will, my lord.
 Leontes. Thou want'st a rough pash and the shoots that
   I have,
To be full like me: yet they say we are
Almost as like as eggs; women say so   130
(That will say any thing!) but were they false
As o'er-dyed blacks, as wind, as waters; false
As dice are to be wished, by one that fixes
No bourn 'twixt his and mine; yet were it true
To say this boy were like me....Come, sir page,
Look on me with your welkin eye: sweet villain!
Most dear'st! my collop! Can thy dam?—may't be?
   [*Hermione and Polixenes draw within hearing*
Affection! thy intention stabs the centre:
Thou dost make possible things not so held,
Communicat'st with dreams—how can this be?—   140
With what's unreal thou coactive art,
And fellow'st nothing: then 'tis very credent
Thou mayst co-join with something, and thou dost
(And that beyond commission) and I find it,

(And that to the infection of my brains,
And hard'ning of my brows.)   [*he muses*

  Polixenes.   What means Sicilia?

  Hermione. He something seems unsettled.

  Polixenes [*his hand on Leontes' shoulder*]. How, my lord!

  Leontes [*rouses*]. What cheer? how is't with you, best
    brother?

  Hermione.   You look
As if you held a brow of much distraction:
150 Are you moved, my lord?

  Leontes.   No, in good earnest.
How sometimes nature will betray its folly!
Its tenderness! and make itself a pastime
To harder bosoms! Looking on the lines
Of my boy's face, methoughts I did recoil
Twenty-three years, and saw myself unbreeched,
In my green velvet coat; my dagger muzzled
Lest it should bite its master, and so prove
(As ornaments oft do) too dangerous...
How like, methought, I then was to this kernel,
160 This squash, this gentleman. Mine honest friend,
Will you take eggs for money?

  Mamillius. No, my lord, I'll fight.

  Leontes. You will? why, happy man be's dole! My
    brother,
Are you so fond of your young prince, as we
Do seem to be of ours?

  Polixenes.   If at home, sir,
He's all my exercise, my mirth, my matter:
Now my sworn friend, and then mine enemy;
My parasite, my soldier, statesman, all:
He makes a July's day short as December;
170 And with his varying childness cures in me
Thoughts that would thick my blood.

Leontes.   So stands this squire
Officed with me: we two will walk, my lord,
And leave you to your graver steps....Hermione,
How thou lov'st us, show in our brother's welcome;
Let what is dear in Sicily be cheap:
Next to thyself and my young rover, he's
Apparent to my heart.

Hermione.   If you would seek us,
We are yours i'th' garden: shall's attend you there?

                              [*they move off*

Leontes. To your own bents dispose you: you'll be
          found,
Be you beneath the sky...[*aside*] I am angling now,   180
Though you perceive me not how I give line.

             [*they pause at the door laughing at some jest*
Go to, go to!
How she holds up the neb! the bill to him!
And arms her with the boldness of a wife
To her allowing husband! [*they go out*] Gone already,
Inch-thick, knee-deep! O'er head and ears a forked
          one....
Go, play, boy, play: thy mother plays, and I
Play too; but so disgraced a part, whose issue
Will hiss me to my grave: contempt and clamour
Will be my knell....Go, play, boy, play. There have
          been   190
(Or I am much deceived) cuckolds ere now,
And many a man there is (even at this present,
Now, while I speak this) holds his wife by th'arm,
That little thinks she has been sluiced in's absence,
And his pond fished by his next neighbour (by
Sir Smile, his neighbour): nay, there's comfort in't,
Whiles other men have gates, and those gates opened,
As mine, against their will. Should all despair

That have revolted wives, the tenth of mankind
200 Would hang themselves. Physic for't there's none:
It is a bawdy planet, that will strike
Where 'tis predominant; and 'tis powerful...think it...
From east, west, north, and south! be it concluded,
No barricado for a belly....know't,
It will let in and out the enemy,
With bag and baggage...many thousand on's
Have the disease, and feel't not....How now, boy?
   Mamillius. I am like you, they say.
   Leontes.   Why, that's some comfort.
What! Camillo there?
210 *Camillo* [*comes forward*]. Ay, my good lord.
   Leontes. Go play, Mamillius. Thou'rt an honest man...
                          [*the boy runs off*
Camillo, this great sir will yet stay longer.
   Camillo. You had much ado to make his anchor hold,
When you cast out, it still came home.
   Leontes.   Didst note it?
   Camillo. He would not stay at your petitions, made
His business more material.
   Leontes.   Didst perceive it?
                [*aside, striking his forehead*
They're here with me already; whisp'ring, rounding:
'Sicilia is a—so-forth': 'tis far gone,
When I shall gust it last....How came't, Camillo,
220 That he did stay?
   Camillo.   At the good queen's entreaty.
   Leontes. At the queen's be't: 'good,' should be per-
          tinent,
But so it is, it is not. Was this taken
By any understanding pate but thine?
For thy conceit is soaking, will draw in
More than the common blocks....not noted, is't,

But of the finer natures? by some severals
Of head-piece extraordinary? lower messes
Perchance are to this business purblind? say.

Camillo. Business, my lord? I think most understand
Bohemia stays here longer.

Leontes.   Ha!

Camillo.   Stays here longer.   230

Leontes. Ay, but why?

Camillo. To satisfy your highness, and the entreaties
Of our most gracious mistress.

Leontes.   Satisfy?
Th'entreaties of your mistress? satisfy?
Let that suffice....I have trusted thee, Camillo,
With all the nearest things to my heart, as well
My chamber-counsels, wherein, priest-like, thou
Hast cleansed my bosom; ay, from thee departed
Thy penitent reformed: but we have been
Deceived in thy integrity, deceived   240
In that which seems so.

Camillo.   Be it forbid, my lord!

Leontes. To bide upon't: thou art not honest: or,
If thou inclin'st that way, thou art a coward,
Which hoxes honesty behind, restraining
From course required: or else thou must be counted
A servant, grafted in my serious trust,
And therein negligent; or else a fool,
That seest a game played home, the rich stake drawn,
And tak'st it all for jest.

Camillo.   My gracious lord,
I may be negligent, foolish, and fearful—   250
In every one of these no man is free,
But that his negligence, his folly, fear,
Among the infinite doings of the world,
Sometime puts forth. In your affairs, my lord,

If ever I were wilful-negligent,
It was my folly; if industriously
I played the fool, it was my negligence,
Not weighing well the end; if ever fearful
To do a thing, where I the issue doubted,
260 Whereof the execution did cry out
Against the non-performance, 'twas a fear
Which oft infects the wisest: these, my lord,
Are such allowed infirmities, that honesty
Is never free of. But, beseech your grace,
Be plainer with me, let me know my trespass
By its own visage: if I then deny it,
'Tis none of mine.

    Leontes.   Ha' not you seen, Camillo
(But that's past doubt: you have, or your eye-glass
Is thicker than a cuckold's horn), or heard
270 (For to a vision so apparent rumour
Cannot be mute) or thought (for cogitation
Resides not in that man that does not think)
My wife is slippery? If thou wilt confess,
Or else be impudently negative,
To have nor eyes, nor ears, nor thought, then say
My wife's a hobby-horse, deserves a name
As rank as any flax-wench that puts to
Before her troth-plight: say't, and justify't.

    Camillo. I would not be a stander-by, to hear
280 My sovereign mistress clouded so, without
My present vengeance taken: 'shrew my heart,
You never spoke what did become you less
Than this; which to reiterate, were sin
As deep as that, though true.

    Leontes.   Is whispering nothing?
Is leaning cheek to cheek? is meeting noses?
Kissing with inside lip? stopping the career

Of laughter with a sigh (a note infallible
Of breaking honesty)? horsing foot on foot?
Skulking in corners? wishing clocks more swift?
Hours, minutes? noon, midnight? and all eyes   290
Blind with the pin and web but theirs; theirs only,
That would unseen be wicked? Is this nothing?
Why then the world, and all that's in't, is nothing,
The covering sky is nothing, Bohemia nothing,
My wife is nothing, nor nothing have these nothings,
If this be nothing.
  Camillo.   Good my lord, be cured
Of this diseased opinion, and betimes,
For 'tis most dangerous.
  Leontes.   Say it be, 'tis true.
  Camillo. No, no, my lord.
  Leontes.   It is; you lie, you lie:
I say thou liest, Camillo, and I hate thee,   300
Pronounce thee a gross lout, a mindless slave,
Or else a hovering temporizer, that
Canst with thine eyes at once see good and evil,
Inclining to them both: were my wife's liver
Infected as her life, she would not live
The running of one glass.
  Camillo.   Who does infect her?
  Leontes. Why, he that wears her like her medal, hanging
About his neck—Bohemia! who, if I
Had servants true about me, that bare eyes
To see alike mine honour, as their profits   310
(Their own particular thrifts) they would do that
Which should undo more doing: ay, and thou
His cupbearer, whom I from meaner form
Have benched and reared to worship, who mayst see
Plainly as heaven sees earth and earth sees heaven,
How I am galled, mightst bespice a cup,

To give mine enemy a lasting wink;
Which draught to me, were cordial.
 Camillo.   Sir, my lord,
I could do this, and that with no rash potion,
320 But with a ling'ring dram, that should not work
Maliciously like poison: but I cannot
Believe this crack to be in my dread mistress
(So sovereignly being honourable!)
†T'have loved the—
 Leontes.   Make that thy question, and go rot!
Dost think I am so muddy, so unsettled,
To appoint myself in this vexation, sully
The purity and whiteness of my sheets
(Which to preserve is sleep, which being spotted
Is goads, thorns, nettles, tails of wasps),
330 Give scandal to the blood o'th' prince my son
(Who I do think is mine, and love as mine),
Without ripe moving to't? Would I do this?
Could man so blench?
 Camillo.   I must believe you, sir,
I do, and will fetch off Bohemia for't:
Provided, that when he's removed, your highness
Will take again your queen, as yours at first,
†Even for your son's sake, and thereby forestalling
The injury of tongues in courts and kingdoms
Known and allied to yours.
 Leontes.   Thou dost advise me,
340 Even so as I mine own course have set down:
I'll give no blemish to her honour, none.
 Camillo. My lord,
Go then; and with a countenance as clear
As friendship wears at feasts, keep with Bohemia,
And with your queen...I am his cupbearer,
If from me he have wholesome beverage,

Account me not your servant.
 Leontes.   This is all:
Do't, and thou hast the one half of my heart;
Do't not, thou split'st thine own.
 Camillo.   I'll do't, my lord.
 Leontes. I will seem friendly, as thou hast advised me. 350
          [*he goes out*

 Camillo. O miserable lady....But, for me,
What case stand I in? I must be the poisoner
Of good Polixenes, and my ground to do't
Is the obedience to a master; one,
Who in rebellion with himself, will have
All that are his, so too....To do this deed,
Promotion follows...If I could find example
Of thousands that had struck anointed kings
And flourished after, I'ld not do't: but since
Nor brass, nor stone, nor parchment, bears not one,   360
Let villainy itself forswear't....I must
Forsake the court: to do't, or no, is certain
To me a break-neck....Happy star reign now!
Here comes Bohemia.

POLIXENES enters, perplexed

 (*Polixenes.*   This is strange: methinks
My favour here begins to warp. Not speak!
         [*he sees Camillo*
Good day, Camillo.
 Camillo.   Hail, most royal sir!
 Polixenes. What is the news i'th' court?
 Camillo.   None rare, my lord.
 Polixenes. The king hath on him such a countenance
As he had lost some province, and a region
Loved as he loves himself: even now I met him   370
With customary compliment, when he,

Wafting his eyes to th' contrary, and falling
A lip of much contempt, speeds from me, and
So leaves me, to consider what is breeding
That changes thus his manners.

   Camillo. I dare not know, my lord.

   Polixenes. How! dare not? do not. Do you know, and
      dare not?
Be intelligent to me—'tis thereabouts:
For, to yourself, what you do know, you must,
380 And cannot say you dare not....Good Camillo,
Your changed complexions are to me a mirror,
Which shows me mine changed too: for I must be
A party in this alteration, finding
Myself thus altered with't.

   Camillo.   There is a sickness
Which puts some of us in distemper, but
I cannot name the disease, and it is caught
Of you, that yet are well.

   Polixenes.   How! caught of me?
Make me not sighted like the basilisk:
I have looked on thousands, who have sped the better
390 By my regard, but killed none so...Camillo—
As you are certainly a gentleman, thereto
Clerk-like experienced, which no less adorns
Our gentry than our parents' noble names,
In whose success we are gentle—I beseech you,
If you know aught which does behove my knowledge
Thereof to be informed, imprison't not
In ignorant concealment.

   Camillo.   I may not answer.

   Polixenes. A sickness caught of me, and yet I well!
I must be answered....Dost thou hear, Camillo,
400 I conjure thee, by all the parts of man
Which honour does acknowledge, whereof the least

Is not this suit of mine, that thou declare
What incidency thou dost guess of harm
Is creeping toward me; how far off, how near;
Which way to be prevented, if to be;
If not, how best to bear it.

 Camillo.   Sir, I will tell you,
Since I am charged in honour and by him
That I think honourable: therefore mark my counsel,
Which must be even as swiftly followed, as
I mean to utter it; or both yourself and me   410
Cry 'lost,' and so good night!

 Polixenes.   On, good Camillo.
 Camillo. I am appointed him to murder you.
 Polixenes. By whom, Camillo?
 Camillo.   By the king.
 Polixenes.   For what!
 Camillo. He thinks, nay with all confidence he swears,
As he had seen't, or been an instrument
To vice you to't, that you have touched his queen
Forbiddenly.

 Polixenes. O, then my best blood turn
To an infected jelly, and my name
Be yoked with his that did betray the Best!
Turn then my freshest reputation to   420
A savour that may strike the dullest nostril
Where I arrive, and my approach be shunned,
Nay hated too, worse than the great'st infection
That e'er was heard or read!

 Camillo.   †Swear this thought over
By each particular star in heaven and
By all their influences! you may as well
Forbid the sea for to obey the moon,
As or by oath remove or counsel shake
The fabric of his folly, whose foundation

430 Is piled upon his faith, and will continue
The standing of his body.
    Polixenes.   How should this grow?
    Camillo. I know not: but I am sure 'tis safer to
Avoid what's grown than question how 'tis born.
If therefore you dare trust my honesty,
That lies encloséd in this trunk which you
Shall bear along impawned, away to-night!
Your followers I will whisper to the business,
And will by twos and threes, at several posterns,
Clear them o'th' city: for myself, I'll put
440 My fortunes to your service, which are here
By this discovery lost....Be not uncertain,
For by the honour of my parents I
Have uttered truth: which if you seek to prove,
I dare not stand by; nor shall you be safer
Than one condemned by the king's own mouth:
Thereon his execution sworn.
    Polixenes.   I do believe thee:
I saw his heart in's face....Give me thy hand,
Be pilot to me, and thy places shall
Still neighbour mine. My ships are ready, and
450 My people did expect my hence departure
Two days ago....This jealousy
Is for a precious creature: as she's rare,
Must it be great; and, as his person's mighty,
Must it be violent; and as he does conceive
He is dishonoured by a man which ever
Professed to him, why, his revenges must
In that be made more bitter. Fear o'ershades me:
Good expedition be my friend, and comfort
The gracious queen, part of his theme, but nothing
460 Of his ill-ta'en suspicion! Come, Camillo,
I will respect thee as a father, if

Thou bear'st my life off. Hence: let us avoid.

Camillo. It is in mine authority to command
The keys of all the posterns: please your highness
To take the urgent hour....Come, sir, away.   [*they go*

Some hours pass

[2. 1.] HERMIONE *enters with her ladies and* MAMIL-
LIUS: *they sit, the Queen and some of the ladies at one
end of the gallery, the rest at the other*

Hermione. Take the boy to you: he so troubles me,
'Tis past enduring.

1 *Lady.*   Come, my gracious lord,
Shall I be your playfellow?

Mamillius.   No, I'll none of you.

1 *Lady.* Why, my sweet lord?

Mamillius. You'll kiss me hard, and speak to me as if
I were a baby still....I love you better.

2 *Lady.* And why so, my lord?

Mamillius.   Not for because
Your brows are blacker; yet black brows, they say,
Become some women best, so that there be not
Too much hair there, but in a semicircle,   10
Or a half-moon made with a pen.

2 *Lady.*   Who taught' this?

Mamillius. I learned it out of women's faces....Pray now
What colour are your eyebrows?

1 *Lady.*   Blue, my lord.

Mamillius. Nay, that's a mock: I have seen a lady's nose
That has been blue, but not her eyebrows.

1 *Lady.*   Hark ye,
The queen your mother rounds apace: we shall
Present our services to a fine new prince
One of these days, and then you'ld wanton with us,
If we would have you.

2 *Lady*.   She is spread of late

20 Into a goodly bulk (good time encounter her!)

Hermione. What wisdom stirs amongst you? Come, sir,
now
I am for you again: pray you, sit by us,
And tell's a tale.

Mamillius [*comes over*]. Merry, or sad, shall't be?

Hermione. As merry as you will.

Mamillius. A sad tale's best for winter: I have one
Of sprites and goblins.

Hermione.   Let's have that, good sir.
Come on, sit down, come on, and do your best
To fright me with your sprites: you're powerful at it.

Mamillius. There was a man—

Hermione.   Nay, come, sit down; then on.
                              [*he climbs upon her knee*

30 *Mamillius*. Dwelt by a churchyard...I will tell it softly,
Yon crickets shall not hear it.

Hermione.   Come on then,
And give't me in mine ear.   [*they whisper together*

LEONTES *enters, with* ANTIGONUS, *lords and a guard;*
he pauses near the door

Leontes. Was he met there? his train? Camillo with him?

1 *Lord*. Behind the tuft of pines I met them, never
Saw I men scour so on their way: I eyed them
Even to their ships.

Leontes.   How blest am I
In my just censure! in my true opinion!
Alack, for lesser knowledge! how accursed,
In being so blest! There may be in the cup

40 A spider steeped, and one may drink, depart,
And yet partake no venom (for his knowledge
Is not infected): but if one present

Th'abhorred ingredient to his eye, make known
How he hath drunk, he cracks his gorge, his sides,
With violent hefts: I have drunk, and seen the spider....
Camillo was his help in this, his pandar:
There is a plot against my life, my crown;
All's true that is mistrusted: that false villain
Whom I employed was pre-employed by him:
He has discovered my design, and I   50
Remain a pinched thing; yea, a very trick
For them to play at will...How came the posterns
So easily open?
    1 *Lord*.   By his great authority,
Which often hath no less prevailed than so
On your command.
    Leontes.   I know't too well....
        [*coming forward, he roughly snatches up Mamillius
            from Hermione's lap*
Give me the boy, I am glad you did not nurse him:
Though he does bear some signs of me, yet you
Have too much blood in him.
    Hermione.   What is this? sport?
    Leontes. Bear the boy hence, he shall not come about her,
Away with him! and let her sport herself   60
With that she's big with—for 'tis Polixenes
Has made thee swell thus.
    Hermione.   But I'ld say he had not,
And I'll be sworn you would believe my saying,
Howe'er you lean to th' nayward. [*they carry the boy away*
    Leontes.   You, my lords,
Look on her, mark her well; be but about
To say 'she is a goodly lady,' and
The justice of your hearts will thereto add
''Tis pity she's not honest...honourable':
Praise her but for this her without-door form

70 (Which on my faith deserves high speech) and straight
The shrug, the hum or ha!—these petty brands
That calumny doth use; O, I am out,
That mercy does, for calumny will sear
Virtue itself—these shrugs, these hums, and ha's,
When you have said 'she's goodly,' come between
Ere you can say 'she's honest': but be't known,
(From him that has most cause to grieve it should be)
She's an adultress.
    Hermione.   Should a villain say so
(The most replenished villain in the world),
80 He were as much more villain...You, my lord,
Do but mistake.
    Leontes.   You have mistook, my lady,
Polixenes for Leontes: O thou thing!
Which I'll not call a creature of thy place,
Lest barbarism, making me the precedent,
Should a like language use to all degrees,
And mannerly distinguishment leave out
Betwixt the prince and beggar: I have said
She's an adultress, I have said with whom:
More; she's a traitor, and Camillo is
90 A fedary with her, and one that knows
What she should shame to know herself
But with her most vile principal...that she's
A bed-swerver, even as bad as those
That vulgars give bold'st titles; ay, and privy
To this their late escape.
    Hermione.   No, by my life,
Privy to none of this...How will this grieve you,
When you shall come to clearer knowledge, that
You thus have published me? Gentle my lord,
You scarce can right me throughly then, to say
100 You did mistake.

Leontes.   No: if I mistake
In those foundations which I build upon,
The Centre is not big enough to bear
A school-boy's top....Away with her to prison:
He who shall speak for her is afar off guilty,
But that he speaks.
   Hermione.   There's some ill planet reigns:
I must be patient, till the heavens look
With an aspect more favourable....Good my lords,
I am not prone to weeping, as our sex
Commonly are, the want of which vain dew
Perchance shall dry your pities: but I have   110
That honourable grief lodged here, which burns
Worse than tears drown: beseech you all, my lords,
With thoughts so qualified as your charities
Shall best instruct you, measure me; and so
The king's will be performed!
   Leontes [*to the guard, stamping his foot*]. Shall I be heard?
   Hermione. Who is't that goes with me? Beseech your
          highness,
My women may be with me, for you see
My plight requires it. Do not weep, good fools,
There is no cause: when you shall know your mistress
Has deserved prison, then abound in tears   120
As I come out: this action I now go on
Is for my better grace....Adieu, my lord!
I never wished to see you sorry, now
I trust I shall....My women come, you have leave.
   Leontes [*to the guard*]. Go, do our bidding; hence.
          [*they lead the Queen away; her ladies follow*
   1 *Lord.* Beseech your highness, call the queen again.
   Antigonus. Be certain what you do, sir, lest your justice
Prove violence, in the which three great ones suffer,
Yourself, your queen, your son.

    1 *Lord.*   For her, my lord,
130 I dare my life lay down and will do't, sir,
Please you t'accept it, that the queen is spotless
I'th'eyes of heaven, and to you—I mean
In this which you accuse her.
    Antigonus.   If it prove
She's otherwise, I'll keep my stables where
I lodge my wife, I'll go in couples with her;
Than when I feel and see her no farther trust her;
For every inch of woman in the world,
Ay, every dram of woman's flesh is false,
If she be.
    Leontes. Hold your peaces.
    1 *Lord.*   Good my lord—
140 *Antigonus.* It is for you we speak, not for ourselves:
You are abused, and by some putter-on
That will be damned for't; would I knew the villain,
†I would lam-damn him…Be she honour-flawed,
I have three daughters; the eldest is eleven;
The second and the third, nine and some five;
If this prove true, they'll pay for't: by mine honour,
I'll geld 'em all; fourteen they shall not see,
To bring false generations: they are co-heirs,
And I had rather glib myself, than they
150 Should not produce fair issue.
    Leontes.   Cease, no more!
You smell this business with a sense as cold
As is a dead man's nose: but I do see't and feel't,
As you feel doing thus…[*he tweaks his nose*] and see withal
The instruments that feel.
    Antigonus.   If it be so,
We need no grave to bury honesty,
There's not a grain of it the face to sweeten
Of the whole dungy earth.

Leontes. What! lack I credit?

1 *Lord.* I had rather you did lack than I, my lord,
Upon this ground: and more it would content me
To have her honour true than your suspicion, 160
Be blamed for't how you might.

Leontes. Why, what need we
Commune with you of this, but rather follow
Our forceful instigation? Our prerogative
Calls not your counsels, but our natural goodness
Imparts this: which if you, or stupefied,
Or seeming so in skill, cannot or will not
Relish a truth like us...inform yourselves
We need no more of your advice: the matter,
The loss, the gain, the ord'ring on't, is all
Properly ours.

Antigonus. And I wish, my liege, 170
You had only in your silent judgement tried it,
Without more overture.

Leontes. How could that be?
Either thou art most ignorant by age,
Or thou wert born a fool...Camillo's flight,
Added to their familiarity
(Which was as gross as ever touched conjecture,
That lacked sight only, nought for approbation
But only seeing, all other circumstances
Made up to th' deed) doth push on this proceeding:
Yet, for a greater confirmation 180
(For in an act of this importance, 'twere
Most piteous to be wild), I have dispatched in post
To sacred Delphos, to Apollo's temple,
Cleomenes and Dion, whom you know
Of stuffed sufficiency: now from the oracle
They will bring all—whose spiritual counsel had,
Shall stop or spur me....Have I done well?

1 Lord. Well done, my lord.

Leontes. Though I am satisfied, and need no more
190 Than what I know, yet shall the oracle
Give rest to th' minds of others; such as he,

[points at Antigonus

Whose ignorant credulity will not
Come up to th' truth....So have we thought it good,
From our free person she should be confined,
Lest that the treachery of the two fled hence
Be left her to perform. Come, follow us,
We are to speak in public; for this business
Will raise us all.

Antigonus.   To laughter, as I take it,
If the good truth were known.   *[they go*

[2. 2.]   *The outer room of a prison in Sicilia*

PAULINA, a gentleman, and attendants enter

Paulina. The keeper of the prison, call to him;
Let him have knowledge who I am....

*[the gentleman goes; Paulina
paces up and down*

Good lady,
No court in Europe is too good for thee,
What dost thou then in prison?

The gentleman returns with the Gaoler.

Now, good sir,
You know me, do you not?

Gaoler [bows].   For a worthy lady,
And one whom much I honour.

Paulina.   Pray you then,
Conduct me to the queen.

Gaoler.   I may not, madam.
To the contrary I have express commandment.

Paulina. Here's ado,
To lock up honesty and honour from   10
Th'access of gentle visitors! Is't lawful, pray you,
To see her women? any of them? Emilia?
  Gaoler. So please you, madam,
To put apart these your attendants, I
Shall bring Emilia forth.
  Paulina.   I pray now, call her...
Withdraw yourselves.   [*the attendants depart*
  Gaoler.   And, madam,
I must be present at your conference.
  Paulina. Well: be't so: prithee.   [*the Gaoler goes*
Here's such ado to make no stain a stain,
As passes colouring....

              The Gaoler returns with EMILIA

                        Dear gentlewoman,   20
How fares our gracious lady?
  Emilia. As well as one so great and so forlorn
May hold together: on her frights and griefs
(Which never tender lady hath borne greater)
She is, something before her time, delivered.
  Paulina. A boy?
  Emilia.   A daughter—and a goodly babe,
Lusty and like to live: the queen receives
Much comfort in't: says, 'My poor prisoner,
I am innocent as you.'
  Paulina.   I dare be sworn...
These dangerous unsafe lunes i'th' king, beshrew them! 30
He must be told on't, and he shall: the office
Becomes a woman best; I'll take't upon me,
If I prove honey-mouthed, let my tongue blister,
And never to my red-looked anger be
The trumpet any more...Pray you, Emilia,

Commend my best obedience to the queen,
If she dares trust me with her little babe,
I'll show't the king and undertake to be
Her advocate to th' loud'st....We do not know
40 How he may soften at the sight o'th' child:
The silence often of pure innocence
Persuades when speaking fails.
    Emilia.   Most worthy madam,
Your honour and your goodness is so evident,
That your free undertaking cannot miss
A thriving issue: there is no lady living
So meet for this great errand...Please your ladyship
To visit the next room, I'll presently
Acquaint the queen of your most noble offer,
Who, but to-day, hammered of this design,
50 But durst not tempt a minister of honour,
Lest she should be denied.
    Paulina.   Tell her, Emilia,
I'll use that tongue I have: if wit flow from't
As boldness from my bosom, let't not be doubted
I shall do good.
    Emilia.   Now be you blest for it!
I'll to the queen: please you, come something nearer.
                             [*she goes*

    Gaoler. Madam, if't please the queen to send the babe,
I know not what I shall incur to pass it,
Having no warrant.
    Paulina.   You need not fear it, sir:
This child was prisoner to the womb, and is
60 By law and process of great nature thence
Freed and enfranchised—not a party to
The anger of the king, nor guilty of
(If any be) the trespass of the queen.
    Gaoler. I do believe it.

Paulina. Do not you fear: upon mine honour, I
Will stand betwixt you and danger. [*they follow Emilia*

[2. 3.]   *The gallery in the palace (as before)*

LEONTES *pacing to and fro alone*

Leontes. Nor night, nor day, no rest: it is but weakness
To bear the matter thus; mere weakness. If
The cause were not in being...part o'th' cause,
She, th'adultress...for the harlot king
Is quite beyond mine arm, out of the blank
And level of my brain: plot-proof: but she
I can hook to me: say that she were gone,
Given to the fire, a moiety of my rest
Might come to me again...[*knocking at the door*]
          Who's there?

A servant enters

Servant.   My lord!
Leontes. How does the boy?
Servant.   He took good rest to-night;   10
'Tis hoped his sickness is discharged.
(*Leontes.* To see his nobleness!
Conceiving the dishonour of his mother,
He straight declined, drooped, took it deeply,
Fastened and fixed the shame on't in himself;
Threw off his spirit, his appetite, his sleep,
And downright languished....[*remembers the servant*]
          Leave me solely: go,
See how he fares...   [*the servant goes*
               Fie, fie! no thought of him—
The very thought of my revenges that way
Recoil upon me: in himself too mighty,   20
And in his parties, his alliance; let him be,
Until a time may serve. For present vengeance,

Take it on her...Camillo and Polixenes
Laugh at me; make their pastime at my sorrow:
They should not laugh if I could reach them, nor
Shall she, within my power. [*he sits, lost in his thoughts*

*PAULINA, with a baby in her arms, enters through the door
at the other end of the gallery, followed swiftly by her
husband ANTIGONUS, lords, and the servant, who try to
prevent her*

   1 *Lord*.   You must not enter.
   Paulina. Nay, rather, good my lords, be second to me:
Fear you his tyrannous passion more, alas,
Than the queen's life? a gracious innocent soul,
30 More free than he is jealous.
   Antigonus.   That's enough.
   2 *Servant*. Madam; he hath not slept to-night, com-
        manded
None should come at him.
   Paulina.   Not so hot, good sir,
I come to bring him sleep....'Tis such as you,
That creep like shadows by him, and do sigh
At each his needless heavings...such as you
Nourish the cause of his awaking. I
Do come with words as medicinal as true;
Honest, as either; to purge him of that humour,
That presses him from sleep.
   Leontes [*turns*].   What noise there, ho?
40 *Paulina*. No noise, my lord, but needful conference,
About some gossips for your highness.
   Leontes.   How!
Away with that audacious lady. Antigonus,
I charged thee that she should not come about me,
I knew she would.
   Antigonus.   I told her so, my lord,
On your displeasure's peril, and on mine,

She should not visit you.

Leontes.　　　　　What! canst not rule her?

Paulina. From all dishonesty he can: in this—
Unless he take the course that you have done,
Commit me for committing honour—trust it,
He shall not rule me.

Antigonus.　　　　La you now! you hear!　　　50
When she will take the rein I let her run,
[*aside*] But she'll not stumble.

Paulina.　　　　　Good my liege, I come...
And I beseech you hear me, who profess
Myself your loyal servant, your physician,
Your most obedient counsellor; yet that dare
Less appear so, in comforting your evils,
Than such as most seem yours....I say, I come
From your good queen.

Leontes. Good queen!

Paulina. Good queen, my lord, good queen, I say
　　　good queen,　　　　　　　　　　　　　60
And would by combat make her good, so were I
A man, the worst about you.

Leontes.　　　　　Force her hence.

Paulina. Let him that makes but trifles of his eyes
First hand me; on mine own accord, I'll off,
But first I'll do my errand. The good queen
(For she is good) hath brought you forth a daughter—
Here 'tis...[*she lays the child before him*] commends it to
　　　your blessing.

Leontes.　　　　　　　　　　Out!
A mankind witch! Hence with her, out o' door:
A most intelligencing bawd!

Paulina.　　　　Not so:
I am as ignorant in that, as you　　　　　　70
In so entitling me: and no less honest

Than you are mad; which is enough, I'll warrant,
As this world goes, to pass for honest.
 Leontes.   Traitors!
Will you not push her out? [*to Antigonus*] Give her the
   bastard,
Thou dotard—thou art woman-tired, unroosted
By thy Dame Partlet here...Take up the bastard,
Take't up, I say; give't to thy crone.
 Paulina.   For ever
Unvenerable be thy hands, if thou
Tak'st up the princess, by that forcéd baseness
80 Which he has put upon't!
 Leontes.   He dreads his wife.
 Paulina. So I would you did; then 'twere past all doubt,
You'ld call your children yours.
 Leontes.   A nest of traitors!
 Antigonus. I am none, by this good light.
 Paulina.   Nor I; nor any
But one that's here; and that's himself: for he
The sacred honour of himself, his queen's,
His hopeful son's, his babe's, betrays to slander,
Whose sting is sharper than the sword's; and will not
(For, as the case now stands, it is a curse
He cannot be compelled to't) once remove
90 The root of his opinion, which is rotten,
As ever oak or stone was sound.
 Leontes.   A callet
Of boundless tongue, who late hath beat her husband,
And now baits me! This brat is none of mine,
It is the issue of Polixenes....
Hence with it, and together with the dam
Commit them to the fire!
 Paulina.   It is yours;
And, might we lay th'old proverb to your charge,

So like you, 'tis the worse. Behold, my lords,
Although the print be little, the whole matter
And copy of the father: eye, nose, lip,   100
The trick of's frown, his forehead, nay, the valley,
The pretty dimples of his chin and cheek; his smiles;
The very mould and frame of hand, nail, finger:
And, thou, good goddess Nature, which hast made it
So like to him that got it, if thou hast
The ordering of the mind too, 'mongst all colours
No yellow in't, lest she suspect, as he does,
Her children not her husband's!
   Leontes.   A gross hag!
And, lozel, thou art worthy to be hanged,
That wilt not stay her tongue.
   Antigonus.   Hang all the husbands 110
That cannot do that feat, you'll leave yourself
Hardly one subject.
   Leontes.   Once more, take her hence.
   Paulina. A most unworthy and unnatural lord
Can do no more.
   Leontes.   I'll ha' thee burnt.
   Paulina.   I care not:
It is an heretic that makes the fire,
Not she which burns in't. I'll not call you tyrant;
But this most cruel usage of your queen
(Not able to produce more accusation
Than your own weak-hinged fancy) something savours
Of tyranny, and will ignoble make you,   120
Yea, scandalous to the world.
   Leontes.   On your allegiance,
Out of the chamber with her! Were I a tyrant,
Where were her life? she durst not call me so,
If she did know me one. Away with her!
                     [*they **make to thrust her forth***

Paulina. I pray you, do not push me, I'll be gone.
Look to your babe, my lord, 'tis yours: Jove send her
A better guiding spirit! What needs these hands?
　　　　　　　　　　　　　[*they lay hold of her*
You, that are thus so tender o'er his follies,
Will never do him good, not one of you.

130 So, so: farewell, we are gone.　　　　　[*she goes*
　　Leontes. Thou, traitor, hast set on thy wife to this.
My child! away with't! Even thou, that hast
A heart so tender o'er it, take it hence,
And see it instantly consumed with fire;
Even thou and none but thou. Take it up straight:
Within this hour bring me word 'tis done,
And by good testimony, or I'll seize thy life,
With what thou else call'st thine...If thou refuse,
And wilt encounter with my wrath, say so;

140 The bastard brains with these my proper hands
Shall I dash out. Go, take it to the fire,
For thou set'st on thy wife.
　　Antigonus.　　　　　　I did not, sir:
These lords, my noble fellows, if they please,
Can clear me in't.
　　Lords.　　　　　We can; my royal liege,
He is not guilty of her coming hither.
　　Leontes. You're liars all.
　　1 *Lord.* Beseech your highness, give us better credit:
We have always truly served you, and beseech'
So to esteem of us: and on our knees we beg

150 (As recompense of our dear services,
Past, and to come) that you do change this purpose,
Which being so horrible, so bloody, must
Lead on to some foul issue [*they fall upon their knees*]...
　　　　We all kneel.
　　Leontes. I am a feather for each wind that blows:

Shall I live on, to see this bastard kneel
And call me father? better burn it now
Than curse it then....But be it: let it live....
It shall not neither....[*to Antigonus*] You, sir, come you
   hither;
You, that have been so tenderly officious
With Lady Margery, your midwife there,   160
To save this bastard's life; for 'tis a bastard,
So sure as this beard's grey....What will you adventure
To save this brat's life?
   Antigonus.   Any thing, my lord,
That my ability may undergo,
And nobleness impose: at least, thus much;
I'll pawn the little blood which I have left
To save the innocent: any thing possible.
   Leontes. It shall be possible...[*draws*] Swear by this
      sword
Thou wilt perform my bidding.
   Antigonus [*his hand upon the hilt*]. I will, my lord.
   Leontes. Mark and perform it: seest thou? for the fail 170
Of any point in't shall not only be
Death to thyself, but to thy lewd-tongued wife
(Whom for this time we pardon). We enjoin thee,
As thou art liege-man to us, that thou carry
This female bastard hence, and that thou bear it
To some remote and desert place, quite out
Of our dominions; and that there thou leave it
(Without more mercy) to it own protection
And favour of the climate: as by strange fortune
It came to us, I do in justice charge thee,   180
On thy soul's peril and thy body's torture,
That thou commend it strangely to some place
Where chance may nurse or end it: take it up.
   Antigonus. I swear to do this; though a present death

Had been more merciful....[*he takes up the child*] Come
    on, poor babe!
Some powerful spirit instruct the kites and ravens
To be thy nurses! Wolves and bears, they say,
Casting their savageness aside, have done
Like offices of pity....Sir, be prosperous
190 In more than this deed does require; and blessing,
Against this cruelty, fight on thy side,
Poor thing, condemned to loss! [*he bears away the child*
    Leontes.   No! I'll not rear
Another's issue.

A servant enters

    Servant.   Please your highness, posts
From those you sent to th'oracle are come
An hour since: Cleomenes and Dion,
Being well arrived from Delphos, are both landed,
Hasting to th' court.
    1 *Lord*.   So please you, sir, their speed
Hath been beyond accompt.
    Leontes.   Twenty three days
They have been absent: 'tis good speed; foretells
200 The great Apollo suddenly will have
The truth of this appear...Prepare you, lords,
Summon a session, that we may arraign
Our most disloyal lady: for as she hath
Been publicly accused, so shall she have
A just and open trial....[*he muses*] While she lives,
My heart will be a burthen to me....Leave me,
And think upon my bidding.   [*they go*

[3. 1.] *Before an inn upon a high road in Sicilia*

CLEOMENES *and* DION, *easing their legs, as they wait for fresh horses*

Cleomenes. The climate's delicate, the air most sweet,
Fertile the isle, the temple much surpassing
The common praise it bears.
Dion.   I shall report,
For most it caught me, the celestial habits
(Methinks I so should term them) and the reverence
Of the grave wearers. O, the sacrifice!
How ceremonious, solemn, and unearthly
It was i'th'off'ring!
Cleomenes.   But of all, the burst
And the ear-deaf'ning voice o'th'oracle,
Kin to Jove's thunder, so surprised my sense,   10
That I was nothing.
Dion.   If th'event o'th' journey
Prove as successful to the queen (O be't so!)
As it hath been to us, rare, pleasant, speedy,
The time is worth the use on't.
Cleomenes.   Great Apollo,
Turn all to th' best! These proclamations,
So forcing faults upon Hermione,
I little like.
Dion.   The violent carriage of it
Will clear or end the business; when the oracle
                    [*he takes a packet from his bosom*
(Thus by Apollo's great divine sealed up)
Shall the contents discover, something rare   20
Even then will rush to knowledge....Go: fresh horses!
And gracious be the issue!   [*they turn back*

[3. 2.] *A Court of Justice; on a platform at the back a chair of state with* LEONTES *seated thereon, his lords and officers about him. A great concourse of people*

Leontes. This sessions (to our great grief we pronounce)
Even pushes 'gainst our heart: the party tried,
The daughter of a king, our wife, and one
Of us too much beloved....Let us be cleared
Of being tyrannous, since we so openly
Proceed in justice, which shall have due course,
Even to the guilt or the purgation...
Produce the prisoner.
    Officer. It is his highness' pleasure, that the queen
10 Appear in person, here in court.

HERMIONE (*pale and stricken*) *is brought in guarded,* PAULINA *and ladies attending. Murmurs of anger and sympathy from the crowd*

    Officer. Silence!
    Leontes. Read the indictment.
    Officer [*reads*]. 'Hermione, queen to the worthy Leontes, King of Sicilia, thou art here accused and arraigned of high treason, in committing adultery with Polixenes, King of Bohemia, and conspiring with Camillo to take away the life of our sovereign lord the king, thy royal husband: the pretence whereof being by circumstances partly laid open, thou, Hermione, contrary to the 20 faith and allegiance of a true subject, didst counsel and aid them, for their better safety, to fly away by night.'
    Hermione. Since what I am to say must be but that
Which contradicts my accusation, and
The testimony on my part no other
But what comes from myself, it shall scarce boot me
To say 'not guilty': mine integrity,

Being counted falsehood, shall, as I express it,
Be so received....But thus, if powers divine
Behold our human actions (as they do),
I doubt not then but innocence shall make   30
False accusation blush, and tyranny
Tremble at patience....You, my lord, best know
(Who least will seem to do so) my past life
Hath been as continent, as chaste, as true,
As I am now unhappy; which is more
Than history can pattern, though devised
And played to take spectators. For behold me,
A fellow of the royal bed, which owe
A moiety of the throne...a great king's daughter,
The mother to a hopeful prince, here standing   40
To prate and talk for life and honour, 'fore
Who please to come and hear. For life, I prize it
As I weigh grief (which I would spare): for honour,
'Tis a derivative from me to mine,
And only that I stand for....I appeal
To your own conscience, sir, before Polixenes
Came to your court, how I was in your grace,
How merited to be so; since he came,
With what encounter so uncurrent I
Have strained t'appear thus: if one jot beyond   50
The bound of honour, or in act or will
That way inclining, hard'ned be the hearts
Of all that hear me, and my near'st of kin
Cry fie upon my grave!
  Leontes.   I ne'er heard yet,
That any of these bolder vices wanted
Less impudence to gainsay what they did,
Than to perform it first.
  Hermione.   That's true enough,
Though 'tis a saying, sir, not due to me.

Leontes. You will not own it.

Hermione.   More than mistress of
60 Which comes to me in name of fault, I must not
At all acknowledge....For Polixenes
(With whom I am accused) I do confess
I loved him, as in honour he required;
With such a kind of love as might become
A lady like me; with a love, even such,
So, and no other, as yourself commanded:
Which not to have done, I think had been in me
Both disobedience and ingratitude
To you, and toward your friend, whose love had
      spoke,
70 Even since it could speak, from an infant, freely,
That it was yours. Now, for conspiracy,
I know not how it tastes, though it be dished
For me to try how: all I know of it,
Is, that Camillo was an honest man;
And why he left your court, the gods themselves
(Wotting no more than I) are ignorant.

Leontes. You knew of his departure, as you know
What you have underta'en to do in's absence.

Hermione. Sir,
80 You speak a language that I understand not:
My life stands in the level of your dreams,
Which I'll lay down.

Leontes.   Your actions are my dreams.
You had a bastard by Polixenes,
And I but dreamed it! As you were past all shame
('Those of your fact are so), so past all truth;
Which to deny, concerns more than avails: for as
Thy brat hath been cast out, like to itself,
No father owning it (which is indeed
More criminal in thee than it) so thou

Shalt feel our justice; in whose easiest passage   90
Look for no less than death.

  Hermione.   Sir, spare your threats:
The bug which you would fright me with I seek:
To me can life be no commodity:
The crown and comfort of my life (your favour)
I do give lost, for I do feel it gone,
But know not how it went. My second joy,
And first-fruits of my body, from his presence
I am barred, like one infectious. My third comfort
(Starred most unluckily!) is from my breast,
The innocent milk in it most innocent mouth,   100
Haled out to murder. Myself on every post
Proclaimed a strumpet: with immodest hatred
The child-bed privilege denied, which 'longs
To women of all fashion. Lastly, hurried
Here, to this place, i'th'open air, before
I have got strength of limit. Now, my liege,
Tell me what blessings I have here alive,
That I should fear to die? Therefore, proceed...
But yet hear this: mistake me not: no life!—
I prize it not a straw—but for mine honour,   110
Which I would free...If I shall be condemned
Upon surmises (all proofs sleeping else
But what your jealousies awake) I tell you,
'Tis rigour and not law....Your honours all,
I do refer me to the oracle;
Apollo be my judge.

  1 Lord.   This your request
Is altogether just: therefore bring forth,
And in Apollo's name, his oracle.   [*officers depart*

  Hermione. The Emperor of Russia was my father:
O that he were alive, and here beholding   120
His daughter's trial! that he did but see

The flatness of my misery; yet with eyes
Of pity, not revenge!

Officers return with CLEOMENES *and* DION

Officer. You here shall swear upon this sword of justice,
That you, Cleomenes and Dion, have
Been both at Delphos, and from thence have brought
This sealed-up oracle, by the hand delivered
Of great Apollo's priest; and that since then
You have not dared to break the holy seal,
130 Nor read the secrets in't.

    Cleomenes, Dion.   All this we swear.

    Leontes. Break up the seals and read.

    Officer [reads]. 'Hermione is chaste, Polixenes blame-
less, Camillo a true subject, Leontes a jealous tyrant, his
innocent babe truly begotten, and the king shall live without an heir, if that which is lost be not found.'

    Lords. Now blessed be the great Apollo!

    Hermione.   Praised!

    Leontes. Hast thou read truth?

    Officer.   Ay, my lord, even so
As it is here set down.

    Leontes. There is no truth at all i'th'oracle:
140 The sessions shall proceed; this is mere falsehood.

A servant enters in great haste

    Servant. My lord the king...the king!

    Leontes.   What is the business?

    Servant. O sir, I shall be hated to report it!
The prince your son, with mere conceit and fear
Of the queen's speed, is gone.

    Leontes.   How! gone!

    Servant.   Is dead.

    Leontes. Apollo's angry, and the heavens themselves

Do strike at my injustice. [*Hermione faints*] How now
    there!
  Paulina. This news is mortal to the queen: look down
And see what death is doing.
  Leontes.   Take her hence:
Her heart is but o'ercharged: she will recover....
I have too much believed mine own suspicion: 150
Beseech you, tenderly apply to her
Some remedies for life....
            [*Paulina and ladies carry Hermione away*
                Apollo, pardon
My great profaneness 'gainst thine oracle!
I'll reconcile me to Polixenes,
New woo my queen, recall the good Camillo,
Whom I proclaim a man of truth, of mercy...
For being transported by my jealousies
To bloody thoughts and to revenge, I chose
Camillo for the minister to poison
My friend Polixenes: which had been done,   160
But that the good mind of Camillo tardied
My swift command; though I with death, and with
Reward, did threaten and encourage him,
Not doing it, and being done; he (most humane,
And filled with honour) to my kingly guest
Unclasped my practice, quit his fortunes here
(Which you knew great) and to the certain hazard
Of all incertainties himself commended,
No richer than his honour...How he glisters
Thorough my rust! and how his piety   170
Does my deeds make the blacker!

PAULINA returns

 Paulina.   Woe the while!
O, cut my lace, lest my heart, cracking it,
Break too!
 1 *Lord.* What fit is this, good lady?
 Paulina. What studied torments, tyrant, hast for me?
What wheels? racks? fires? what flaying? boiling,
In leads or oils? what old or newer torture
Must I receive, whose every word deserves
To taste of thy most worst? Thy tyranny
(Together working with thy jealousies,
180 Fancies too weak for boys, too green and idle
For girls of nine) O, think what they have done,
And then run mad indeed: stark mad! for all
Thy by-gone fooleries were but spices of it.
That thou betray'dst Polixenes, 'twas nothing—
That did but show thee, of a fool, inconstant,
And damnable ingrateful: nor was't much,
Thou wouldst have poisoned good Camillo's honour,
To have him kill a king; poor trespasses,
More monstrous standing by: whereof I reckon
190 The casting forth to crows thy baby-daughter,
To be or none or little; though a devil
Would have shed water out of fire, ere done't:
Nor is't directly laid to thee, the death
Of the young prince, whose honourable thoughts
(Thoughts high for one so tender) cleft the heart
That could conceive a gross and foolish sire
Blemished his gracious dam: this is not, no,
Laid to thy answer: but the last...O lords,
When I have said, cry 'woe!' The queen, the queen,
200 The sweet'st, dear'st creature's dead! and vengeance
  for't

Not dropped down yet.

  1 *Lord*.   The higher powers forbid!

  Paulina. I say she's dead: I'll swear't. If word nor
      oath

Prevail not, go and see: if you can bring

Tincture or lustre in her lip, her eye,

Heat outwardly, or breath within, I'll serve you

As I would do the gods....But, O thou tyrant!

Do not repent these things, for they are heavier

Than all thy woes can stir: therefore betake thee

To nothing but despair....A thousand knees

Ten thousand years together, naked, fasting,   210

Upon a barren mountain, and still winter

In storm perpetual, could not move the gods

To look that way thou wert.

  Leontes.   Go on, go on:

Thou canst not speak too much, I have deserved

All tongues to talk their bitt'rest.

  1 *Lord*.   Say no more;

Howe'er the business goes, you have made fault

I'th' boldness of your speech.

  Paulina.   I am sorry for't;

All faults I make, when I shall come to know them,

I do repent: alas, I have showed too much

The rashness of a woman: he is touched   220

To th' noble heart....What's gone, and what's past help,

Should be past grief: do not receive affliction

At my petition; I beseech you, rather

Let me be punished, that have minded you

Of what you should forget. Now (good my liege!)

Sir, royal sir, forgive a foolish woman:

The love I bore your queen—lo, fool again!

I'll speak of her no more, nor of your children;

I'll not remember you of my own lord,

230 (Who is lost too)…Take your patience to you,
    And I'll say nothing.
    Leontes.   Thou didst speak but well,
    When most the truth; which I receive much better
    Than to be pitied of thee. Prithee, bring me
    To the dead bodies of my queen and son.
    One grave shall be for both; upon them shall
    The causes of their death appear (unto
    Our shame perpetual). Once a day I'll visit
    The chapel where they lie, and tears shed there
    Shall be my recreation. So long as nature
240 Will bear up with this exercise, so long
    I daily vow to use it. Come, and lead me
    To these sorrows.   *[they go*

[3. 3.]   *A desert part of Bohemia near the sea*

    ANTIGONUS carrying the babe, with a mariner

    Antigonus. Thou art perfect then, our ship hath touched upon
    The deserts of Bohemia?
    Mariner.   Ay, my lord, and fear
    We have landed in ill time; the skies look grimly,
    And threaten present blusters. In my conscience,
    The heavens with that we have in hand are angry,
    And frown upon's.
    Antigonus. Their sacred wills be done! Go, get aboard,
    Look to thy bark, I'll not be long before
    I call upon thee.
10 *Mariner.* Make your best haste, and go not
    Too far i'th' land: 'tis like to be loud weather;
    Besides, this place is famous for the creatures
    Of prey that keep upon't.

Antigonus.   Go thou away,
I'll follow instantly.

Mariner.   I am glad at heart
To be so rid o'th' business.   [*he goes*

Antigonus.   Come, poor babe...
I have heard (but not believed) the spirits o'th' dead
May walk again: if such thing be, thy mother
Appeared to me last night; for ne'er was dream
So like a waking. To me comes a creature,
Sometimes her head on one side, some another—   20
I never saw a vessel of like sorrow,
So filled, and so becoming: in pure white robes,
Like very sanctity, she did approach
My cabin where I lay: thrice bowed before me,
And (gasping to begin some speech) her eyes
Became two spouts; the fury spent, anon
Did this break from her. 'Good Antigonus,
Since fate (against thy better disposition)
Hath made thy person for the thrower-out
Of my poor babe according to thine oath,   30
Places remote enough are in Bohemia,
There weep and leave it crying; and for the babe
Is counted lost for ever, Perdita
I prithee call't...For this ungentle business,
Put on thee by my lord, thou ne'er shalt see
Thy wife Paulina more'...and so, with shrieks
She melted into air. Affrighted much,
I did in time collect myself, and thought
This was so, and no slumber...Dreams are toys,
Yet for this once, yea superstitiously,   40
I will be squared by this. I do believe,
Hermione hath suffered death, and that
Apollo would (this being indeed the issue
Of King Polixenes) it should here be laid

(Either for life or death) upon the earth
Of its right father....[*he lays down the child*] Blossom,
 speed thee well!
There lie, and there thy character: there these,
    [*he sets a box and papers beside it*
Which may, if fortune please, both breed thee, pretty,
And still rest thine....[*thunder heard*] The storm begins!
 Poor wretch,
50 That for thy mother's fault art thus exposed
To loss, and what may follow! Weep I cannot,
But my heart bleeds: and most accursed am I,
To be by oath enjoined to this. Farewell!
The day frowns more and more; thou'rt like to have
A lullaby too rough: I never saw
The heavens so dim by day. [*a noise of hunters*] A
 savage clamour!
Well may I get aboard! This is the chase—
I am gone for ever!   ['*Exit pursued by a bear*'

An old Shepherd comes up

 Shepherd. I would there were no age between ten and
60 three-and-twenty, or that youth would sleep out the rest;
for there is nothing in the between but getting wenches
with child, wronging the ancientry, stealing, fighting.
Hark you now! Would any but these boiled-brains of
nineteen and two-and-twenty hunt this weather? They
have scared away two of my best sheep, which I fear the
wolf will sooner find than the master: if any where I have
them, 'tis by the seaside, browsing of ivy....[*seeing the
child*] Good-luck (an't be thy will) what have we here?
Mercy on's, a barne? a very pretty barne! A boy or a
70 child, I wonder?—a pretty one, a very pretty one! Sure,
some scape: though I am not bookish, yet I can read
waiting-gentlewoman in the scape: this has been some

stair-work, some trunk-work, some behind-door-work: they were warmer that got this than the poor thing is here. I'll take it up for pity—yet I'll tarry till my son come; he hollaed but even now....Whoa, ho hoa!

Clown approaches from behind and shouts in his ear

Clown. Hilloa, loa!

Shepherd [*starts*]. What, art so near? If thou'lt see a thing to talk on when thou art dead and rotten, come hither...What ailest thou, man? 80

Clown [*as in a trance*]. I have seen two such sights, by sea and by land! but I am not to say it is a sea, for it is now the sky—betwixt the firmament and it you cannot thrust a bodkin's point.

Shepherd. Why, boy, how is it?

Clown. I would you did but see how it chafes, how it rages, how it takes up the shore! but that's not to the point...O, the most piteous cry of the poor souls! sometimes to see 'em, and not to see 'em: now the ship boring the moon with her main-mast, and anon swallowed with 90 yeast and froth, as you'ld thrust a cork into a hogshead.... And then for the land-service! to see how the bear tore out his shoulder-bone, how he cried to me for help, and said his name was Antigonus, a nobleman...But to make an end of the ship—to see how the sea flap-dragoned it: but first, how the poor souls roared, and the sea mocked them: and how the poor gentleman roared, and the bear mocked him, both roaring louder than the sea or weather.

Shepherd. Name of mercy, when was this, boy?

Clown. Now, now: I have not winked since I saw these 100 sights: the men are not yet cold under water, nor the bear half dined on the gentleman: he's at it now.

Shepherd. Would I had been by, to have helped the old man!

(*Clown.* I would you had been by the ship side, to have
helped her; there your charity would have lacked footing.

Shepherd. Heavy matters, heavy matters...but look
thee here, boy. Now bless thyself; thou met'st with things
dying, I with things new-born. Here's a sight for thee;
110 look thee, a bearing-cloth for a squire's child! [*points to
the box*] look thee here, take up, take up, boy; open't...
So, let's see, it was told me I should be rich by the fairies.
This is some changeling...Open't: what's within, boy?

Clown [*opens the box*]. You're a made old man; if the
sins of your youth are forgiven you, you're well to live.
Gold! all gold!

Shepherd. This is fairy gold, boy, and 'twill prove so:
up with't, keep it close; home, home, the next way. We
are lucky, boy, and to be so still requires nothing but
120 secrecy. Let my sheep go: come, good boy, the next way
home.

Clown. Go you the next way with your findings. I'll
go see if the bear be gone from the gentleman, and how
much he hath eaten: they are never curst but when they
are hungry: if there be any of him left, I'll bury it.

Shepherd. That's a good deed: if thou mayest discern by
that which is left of him, what he is, fetch me to th' sight
of him.

Clown. Marry, will I; and you shall help to put him
130 i'th' ground.

Shepherd. 'Tis a lucky day, boy, and we'll do good
deeds on't.   [*they go*

[4. 1.]   '*Enter TIME, the Chorus*'

Time. I that please some, try all: both joy and terror
Of good and bad, that makes and unfolds error.
Now take upon me, in the name of Time,
To use my wings...Impute it not a crime

To me, or my swift passage, that I slide
O'er sixteen years, and leave the growth untried
Of that wide gap, since it is in my power
To o'erthrow law and in one self-born hour
To plant and o'erwhelm custom. Let me pass—
The same I am, ere ancient'st order was,   10
Or what is now received: I witness to
The times that brought them in, so shall I do
To th' freshest things now reigning, and make stale
The glistering of this present, as my tale
Now seems to it...Your patience this allowing,
I turn my glass, and give my scene such growing,
As you had slept between: Leontes leaving—
Th'effects of his fond jealousies so grieving
That he shuts up himself—imagine me,
Gentle spectators, that I now may be   20
In fair Bohemia, and remember well
I mentioned a son o'th' king's, which Florizel
I now name to you; and with speed so pace
To speak of Perdita, now grown in grace
Equal with wond'ring: what of her ensues,
I list not prophesy; but let Time's news
Be known when 'tis brought forth. A shepherd's
        daughter,
And what to her adheres, which follows after,
Is th'argument of Time: of this allow,
If ever you have spent time worse ere now;   30
If never, yet that Time himself doth say
He wishes earnestly you never may.   [exit

[4. 2.] *Bohemia. A room in the palace of Polixenes*

POLIXENES and CAMILLO

Polixenes. I pray thee, good Camillo, be no more importunate: 'tis a sickness denying thee any thing; a death to grant this.

Camillo. It is fifteen years since I saw my country: though I have, for the most part, been aired abroad, I desire to lay my bones there. Besides, the penitent king, my master, hath sent for me, to whose feeling sorrows I might be some allay (or I o'erween to think so) which is another spur to my departure.

10 *Polixenes.* As thou lov'st me, Camillo, wipe not out the rest of thy services by leaving me now: the need I have of thee, thine own goodness hath made; better not to have had thee than thus to want thee: thou, having made me businesses, which none without thee can sufficiently manage, must either stay to execute them thyself, or take away with thee the very services thou hast done: which if I have not enough considered (as too much I cannot), to be more thankful to thee shall be my study, and my profit therein the heaping friendships. Of 20 that fatal country Sicilia prithee speak no more, whose very naming punishes me with the remembrance of that penitent, as thou call'st him, and reconciled king, my brother, whose loss of his most precious queen and children are even now to be afresh lamented. Say to me, when saw'st thou the Prince Florizel my son? Kings are no less unhappy, their issue not being gracious, than they are in losing them when they have approved their virtues.

Camillo. Sir, it is three days since I saw the prince: 30 what his happier affairs may be, are to me unknown: but I have (missingly) noted he is of late much retired from court, and is less frequent to his princely exercises than formerly he hath appeared.

Polixenes. I have considered so much, Camillo, and with some care—so far that I have eyes under my service which look upon his removedness: from whom I have this intelligence, that he is seldom from the house of a most homely shepherd; a man, they say, that from very nothing, and beyond the imagination of his neighbours, is grown into an unspeakable estate. 40

Camillo. I have heard, sir, of such a man, who hath a daughter of most rare note: the report of her is extended more than can be thought to begin from such a cottage.

Polixenes. That's likewise part of my intelligence: but, I fear, the angle that plucks our son thither. Thou shalt accompany us to the place, where we will (not appearing what we are) have some question with the shepherd; from whose simplicity I think it not uneasy to get the cause of my son's resort thither. Prithee, be my present partner in this business, and lay aside the thoughts of 50 Sicilia.

Camillo. I willingly obey your command.

Polixenes. My best Camillo! We must disguise ourselves.

[*they go*

[4. 3.] *Bohemia. A field-path leading to a stile, hard by the Shepherd's cottage*

AUTOLYCUS, *clad in a ragged frieze jerkin, comes across the meadow, singing blithely; then pauses by the stile, leaning upon his staff*

> When daffodils begin to peer,
>   With, heigh! the doxy over the dale,
> Why then comes in the sweet o'the year,
>   For the red blood reigns in the winter's pale.

The white sheet bleaching on the hedge,
    With hey! the sweet birds, O how they sing:
Doth set my pugging tooth on edge,
    For a quart of ale is a dish for a king.

The lark, that tirra-lyra chants,
10   With heigh! with hey! the thrush and the jay:
Are summer songs for me and my aunts,
    While we lie tumbling in the hay.

I have served Prince Florizel, and in my time wore three-pile, but now I am out of service.

But shall I go mourn for that, my dear?
    The pale moon shines by night:
And when I wander here and there,
    I then do most go right.

If tinkers may have leave to live,
20   And bear the sow-skin budget,
Then my account I well may give,
    And in the stocks avouch it.

My traffic is sheets: when the kite builds, look to lesser linen. My father named me Autolycus, who being, as I am, littered under Mercury, was likewise a snapper-up of unconsidered trifles...[*points to his rags*] With die and drab I purchased this caparison, and my revenue is the silly cheat. Gallows and knock are too powerful on the highway: beating and hanging are terrors to me: for 30 the life to come, I sleep out the thought of it. A prize! a prize!   [*he hides behind a bush*

CLOWN *appears the other side of the stile*

    Clown [*mounts and sits thereon*]. Let me see—every 'leven wether tods, every tod yields pound and odd shilling: fifteen hundred shorn—what comes the wool to? (*Autolycus.* If the springe hold, the cock's mine.

Clown. I cannot do't without counters....Let me see, what am I to buy for our sheep-shearing feast? Three pound of sugar, five pound of currants, rice...what will this sister of mine do with rice? but my father hath made her Mistress of the Feast, and she lays it on. She hath made 40 me four and twenty nosegays for the shearers—three-man song-men all, and very good ones; but they are most of them means and bases: but one puritan amongst them, and he sings psalms to hornpipes....I must have saffron to colour the warden pies: mace: dates, none; that's out of my note: nutmegs, seven; a race or two of ginger—but that I may beg: four pound of prunes, and as many of raisins o'th' sun.

Autolycus [*staggers forward and falls upon the ground*].
     O, that ever I was born!

Clown. I'th' name of me!   50

Autolycus. O, help me, help me! pluck but off these rags; and then, death, death!

Clown. Alack, poor soul! thou hast need of more rags to lay on thee, rather than have these off.

Autolycus. O, sir, the loathsomeness of them offends me more than the stripes I have received, which are mighty ones and millions.

Clown. Alas, poor man! a million of beating may come to a great matter.

Autolycus. I am robbed, sir, and beaten; my money 60 and apparel ta'en from me, and these detestable things put upon me.

Clown. What, by a horseman or a footman?

Autolycus. A footman, sweet sir, a footman.

Clown. Indeed, he should be a footman, by the garments he has left with thee; if this be a horseman's coat, it hath seen very hot service. Lend me thy hand, I'll help thee: come, lend me thy hand.   [*he lifts him up*

Autolycus [*groans*]. O, good sir, tenderly, O!

70   *Clown*. Alas, poor soul.

Autolycus. O, good sir, softly, good sir: I fear, sir, my
shoulder-blade is out.   [*he leans hard upon him*

Clown. How now? canst stand?

Autolycus. Softly, dear sir...[*picking his pocket*] good
sir, softly...you ha' done me a charitable office.

[*he stands from him*

Clown. Dost lack any money? I have a little money for
thee.

Autolycus. No, good sweet sir; no, I beseech you, sir:
I have a kinsman not past three quarters of a mile hence,
80 unto whom I was going; I shall there have money, or any
thing I want...Offer me no money, I pray you—that
kills my heart.

Clown. What manner of fellow was he that robbed you?

Autolycus. A fellow, sir, that I have known to go about
with troll-my-dames: I knew him once a servant of the
prince; I cannot tell, good sir, for which of his virtues it
was, but he was certainly whipped out of the court.

Clown. His vices, you would say; there's no virtue
whipped out of the court: they cherish it to make it stay
90 there; and yet it will no more but abide.

Autolycus. Vices I would say, sir. I know this man
well, he hath been since an ape-bearer, then a process-
server, a bailiff, then he compassed a motion of the Prodi-
gal Son, and married a tinker's wife within a mile where
my land and living lies; and having flown over many
knavish professions, he settled only in rogue: some call
him Autolycus.

Clown. Out upon him! prig, for my life, prig: he
haunts wakes, fairs, and bear-baitings.

100   *Autolycus*. Very true, sir; he, sir, he; that's the rogue
that put me into this apparel.

Clown. Not a more cowardly rogue in all Bohemia; if
you had but looked big, and spit at him, he'ld have run.

Autolycus. I must confess to you, sir, I am no fighter: I am
false of heart that way, and that he knew, I warrant him.

Clown. How do you now?

Autolycus. Sweet sir, much better than I was; I can
stand, and walk: I will even take my leave of you, and
pace softly towards my kinsman's.

Clown. Shall I bring thee on the way?   110

Autolycus. No, good-faced sir, no, sweet sir.

Clown. Then fare thee well, I must go buy spices for
our sheep-shearing.

Autolycus. Prosper you, sweet sir! [*the Clown goes*]
Your purse is not hot enough to purchase your spice: I'll
be with you at your sheep-shearing too: if I make not
this cheat bring out another, and the shearers prove sheep,
let me be unrolled, and my name put in the book of
virtue!

> [*sings*] Jog on, jog on, the foot-path way,   120
> And merrily hent the stile-a:
> A merry heart goes all the day,
> Your sad tires in a mile-a.
>   [*he leaps the stile and passes on*

[4. 4.]   *A room in the Shepherd's cottage; at the
back a deep chimney-corner*

FLORIZEL *and* PERDITA, *dressed for the sheep-shearing
festival; she, as Flora, in a flowery gown and with a garland on her head, he as her attendant swain*

Florizel. These your unusual weeds to each part of you
Do give a life: no shepherdess, but Flora
Peering in April's front. This your sheep-shearing
Is as a meeting of the petty gods,
And you the queen on't.

Perdita.   Sir...my gracious lord,
To chide at your extremes, it not becomes me:
(O, pardon, that I name them!) Your high self,
The gracious mark o'th' land, you have obscured
With a swain's wearing; and me (poor lowly maid)
10 Most goddess-like pranked up...But that our feasts
In every mess have folly and the feeders
Digest it with a custom, I should blush
†To see you so attired; swoon, I think,
To show myself a glass.
      Florizel.   I bless the time
When my good falcon made her flight across
Thy father's ground.
      Perdita.   Now Jove afford you cause!
To me the difference forges dread (your greatness
Hath not been used to fear): even now I tremble
To think your father, by some accident,
20 Should pass this way, as you did: O the Fates!
How would he look, to see his work, so noble,
Vilely bound up? What would he say? Or how
Should I (in these my borrowed flaunts) behold
The sternness of his presence?
      Florizel.   Apprehend
Nothing but jollity: the gods themselves
(Humbling their deities to love) have taken
The shapes of beasts upon them: Jupiter
Became a bull, and bellowed; the green Neptune
A ram, and bleated; and the fire-robed god,
30 Golden Apollo, a poor humble swain,
As I seem now....Their transformations
Were never for a piece of beauty rarer,
Nor in a way so chaste: since my desires
Run not before mine honour; nor my lusts
Burn hotter than my faith.

Perdita.   O but, sir,
Your resolution cannot hold, when 'tis
Opposed (as it must be) by th' power of the king:
One of these two must be necessities,
Which then will speak, that you must change this purpose,
Or I my life.
  Florizel.   Thou dearest Perdita,   40
With these forced thoughts, I prithee, darken not
The mirth o'th' feast: or I'll be thine, my fair,
Or not my father's: for I cannot be
Mine own, nor any thing to any, if
I be not thine: to this I am most constant,
Though destiny say no. Be merry, gentle,
Strangle such thoughts as these with any thing
That you behold the while....Your guests are coming:
Lift up your countenance, as it were the day
Of celebration of that nuptial which   50
We two have sworn shall come.
  Perdita.   O lady Fortune,
Stand you auspicious!

The SHEPHERD, CLOWN, MOPSA, DORCAS *and others
enter the room, with* POLIXENES *and* CAMILLO, *disguised*

  Florizel.   See, your guests approach,
Address yourself to entertain them sprightly,
And let's be red with mirth.
  Shepherd. Fie, daughter! when my old wife lived, upon
This day she was both pantler, butler, cook,
Both dame and servant: welcomed all, served all:
Would sing her song and dance her turn: now here,
At upper end o'th' table; now i'th' middle:
On his shoulder, and his: her face o'fire   60
With labour, and the thing she took to quench it
She would to each one sip....You are retired,

5   PSWT

As if you were a feasted one, and not
The hostess of the meeting: pray you, bid
These unknown friends to's welcome, for it is
A way to make us better friends, more known:
Come, quench your blushes, and present yourself
That which you are, Mistress o'th' Feast. Come on,
And bid us welcome to your sheep-shearing,
70 As your good flock shall prosper.

    Perdita [*to Polixenes*].   Sir, welcome:
It is my father's will, I should take on me
The hostess-ship o'th' day...[*to Camillo*] You're wel-
    come, sir!
Give me those flowers there, Dorcas....Reverend sirs,
For you there's rosemary and rue—these keep
Seeming and savour all the winter long:
Grace and remembrance be to you both,
And welcome to our shearing!

    Polixenes.   Shepherdess,
(A fair one are you!) well you fit our ages
With flowers of winter.

    Perdita.   Sir, the year growing ancient—
80 Not yet on summer's death nor on the birth
Of trembling winter—the fairest flowers o'th' season
Are our carnations and streaked gillyvors,
Which some call nature's bastards. Of that kind
Our rustic garden's barren, and I care not
To get slips of them.

    Polixenes.   Wherefore, gentle maiden,
Do you neglect them?

    Perdita.   For I have heard it said
There is an art which in their piedness shares
With great creating Nature.

    Polixenes.   Say, there be;
Yet nature is made better by no mean,

But nature makes that mean: so, over that art   90
Which you say adds to nature, is an art
That nature makes...You see, sweet maid, we marry
A gentler scion to the wildest stock,
And make conceive a bark of baser kind
By bud of nobler race. This is an art
Which does mend nature...change it rather, but
The art itself, is nature.

    Perdita [*her eye on Florizel*]. So it is.

    Polixenes. Then make your garden rich in gillyvors,
And do not call them bastards.

    Perdita.   I'll not put
The dibble in earth to set one slip of them: 100
No more than, were I painted, I would wish
This youth should say 'twere well; and only therefore
Desire to breed by me....Here's flowers for you;
Hot lavender, mints, savory, marjoram,
The marigold, that goes to bed with' sun,
And with him rises, weeping; these are flowers
Of middle summer, and I think they are given
To men of middle age...Y'are very welcome.

                     [*she gives them flowers*

    Camillo. I should leave grazing, were I of your flock,
And only live by gazing.

    Perdita.   Out, alas!   110
You'ld be so lean, that blasts of January
Would blow you through and through....[*to Florizel*]
      Now, my fair'st friend,
I would I had some flowers o'th' spring that might
Become your time of day; [*to Mopsa and the other girls*]
      and yours and yours,
That wear upon your virgin branches yet
Your maidenheads growing: O Proserpina,
For the flowers now, that frighted thou let'st fall

From Dis's waggon! daffodils,
That come before the swallow dares, and take
120 The winds of March with beauty; violets (dim,
But sweeter than the lids of Juno's eyes
Or Cytherea's breath); pale primroses,
That die unmarried, ere they can behold
Bright Phœbus in his strength (a malady
Most incident to maids); bold oxlips and
The crown imperial; lilies of all kinds,
The flower-de-luce being one! O, these I lack,
To make you garlands of—and my sweet friend,
To strew him o'er and o'er.

    Florizel.   What, like a corse?

130   *Perdita.* No, like a bank, for love to lie and play on;
Not like a corse: or if...not to be buried,
But quick, and in mine arms. Come, take your flowers,
Methinks I play as I have seen them do
In Whitsun-pastorals: sure this robe of mine
Does change my disposition.

    Florizel.   What you do
Still betters what is done. When you speak, sweet,
I'ld have you do it ever: when you sing,
I'ld have you buy and sell so; so give alms,
Pray so; and for the ord'ring your affairs,
140 To sing them too: when you do dance, I wish you
A wave o'th' sea, that you might ever do
Nothing but that; move still, still so;
And own no other function. Each your doing
(So singular in each particular)
Crowns what you are doing in the present deeds,
That all your acts are queens.

    Perdita.   O Doricles,
Your praises are too large: but that your youth,
And the true blood which peepeth fairly through't,

Do plainly give you out an unstained shepherd,
With wisdom I might fear, my Doricles,   150
You wooed me the false way.

  Florizel.   I think you have
As little skill to fear, as I have purpose
To put you to't....But, come, our dance I pray,
Your hand, my Perdita! so turtles pair,
That never mean to part.

  Perdita.   I'll swear for 'em.

                  [he leads her away for the dance

  Polixenes. This is the prettiest low-born lass that ever
Ran on the green-sward: nothing she does or seems
But smacks of something greater than herself,
Too noble for this place.

  Camillo.   He tells her something
That makes her blood look out: good sooth she is   160
The queen of curds and cream.

  Clown.   Come on: strike up!

  Dorcas. Mopsa must be your mistress: marry, garlic,
To mend her kissing with!

  Mopsa.   Now, in good time!

  Clown. Not a word, a word, we stand upon our manners.
Come, strike up.   *[music*

       '*Here a dance of shepherds and shepherdesses*'

  Polixenes. Pray, good shepherd, what fair swain is this,
Which dances with your daughter?

  Shepherd. They call him Doricles, and boasts himself
To have a worthy feeding: but I have it
Upon his own report, and I believe it;   170
He looks like sooth...He says he loves my daughter,
I think so too; for never gazed the moon
Upon the water, as he'll stand and read
As 'twere my daughter's eyes: and to be plain,

I think there is not half a kiss to choose,
Who loves another best.

Polixenes.   She dances featly.

Shepherd. So she does any thing, though I report it,
That should be silent: if young Doricles
Do light upon her, she shall bring him that
180 Which he not dreams of.

A servant enters

Servant. O master! if you did but hear the pedlar at the
door, you would never dance again after a tabor and
pipe; no, the bagpipe could not move you: he sings
several tunes, faster than you'll tell money: he utters them
as he had eaten ballads, and all men's ears grew to his
tunes.

Clown. He could never come better: he shall come in:
I love a ballad but even too well, if it be doleful matter
merrily set down, or a very pleasant thing indeed and
190 sung lamentably.

Servant. He hath songs for man, or woman, of all
sizes; no milliner can so fit his customers with gloves: he
has the prettiest love-songs for maids, so without bawdry
(which is strange), with such delicate burthens of dildos
and fadings, 'jump her and thump her'; and where some
stretch-mouthed rascal would, as it were, mean mischief,
and break a foul gap into the matter, he makes the maid
to answer, 'Whoop, do me no harm, good man'; puts
him off, slights him, with 'Whoop, do me no harm, good
200 man.'

Polixenes. This is a brave fellow.

Clown. Believe me, thou talkest of an admirable con-
ceited fellow. Has he any unbraided wares?

Servant. He hath ribbons of all the colours i'th' rain-
bow; points, more than all the lawyers in Bohemia can

learnedly handle, though they come to him by th' gross;
inkles, caddisses, cambrics, lawns: why, he sings 'em over,
as they were gods or goddesses; you would think a smock
were a she-angel, he so chants to the sleeve-hand, and the
work about the square on't.   210

Clown. Prithee, bring him in, and let him approach
singing.

Perdita. Forewarn him that he use no scurrilous words
in's tunes.

Clown. You have of these pedlars, that have more in
them than you'ld think, sister.

Perdita. Ay, good brother, or go about to think.

> '*Enter* AUTOLYCUS, *singing,*' *disguised with a
> false beard, and a pack slung open before him*

Lawn as white as driven snow,
Cypress black as e'er was crow,
Gloves as sweet as damask roses,   220
Masks for faces and for noses:
Bugle-bracelet, necklace amber,
Perfume for a lady's chamber:
Golden quoifs and stomachers
For my lads to give their dears:
Pins and poking-sticks of steel,
What maids lack from head to heel:
    Come buy of me, come: come buy, come buy,
    Buy lads, or else your lasses cry:
Come, buy!   230

Clown. If I were not in love with Mopsa, thou shouldst
take no money of me, but being enthralled as I am, it will
also be the bondage of certain ribbons and gloves.

Mopsa. I was promised them against the feast, but they
come not too late now.

Dorcas. He hath promised you more than that, or there be liars.

Mopsa. He hath paid you all he promised you: may be he has paid ycu more, which will shame you to give him 240 again.

Clown. Is there no manners left among maids? will they wear their plackets where they should bear their faces? Is there not milking-time? when you are going to bed? or kill-hole? to whistle off these secrets, but you must be tittle-tattling before all our guests? 'tis well they are whisp'ring: clammer your tongues, and not a word more.

Mopsa. I have done...Come, you promised me a tawdry-lace and a pair of sweet gloves.

Clown. Have I not told thee how I was cozened by the 250 way and lost all my money?

Autolycus. And, indeed, sir, there are cozeners abroad, therefore it behoves men to be wary.

Clown. Fear not thou, man, thou shalt lose nothing here.

Autolycus. I hope so, sir, for I have about me many parcels of charge.

Clown. What hast here? ballads?

Mopsa. Pray now, buy some: I love a ballad in print o' life, for then we are sure they are true.

Autolycus. Here's one, to a very doleful tune, How a 260 usurer's wife was brought to bed of twenty money-bags at a burthen, and how she longed to eat adders' heads and toads carbonadoed.

Mopsa. Is it true, think you?

Autolycus. Very true, and but a month old.

Dorcas. Bless me from marrying a usurer!

Autolycus. Here's the midwife's name to't, one Mistress Tale-porter, and five or six honest wives that were present. Why should I carry lies abroad?

Mopsa. Pray you now, buy it.

Clown. Come on, lay it by: and let's first see moe 270
ballads; we'll buy the other things anon.

Autolycus. Here's another ballad of a fish, that appeared upon the coast, on Wednesday the fourscore of
April, forty thousand fathom above water, and sung this
ballad against the hard hearts of maids: it was thought
she was a woman, and was turned into a cold fish, for she
would not exchange flesh with one that loved her: the
ballad is very pitiful, and as true.

Dorcas. Is it true too, think you?

Autolycus. Five justices' hands at it, and witnesses more 280
than my pack will hold.

Clown. Lay it by too: another.

Autolycus. This is a merry ballad, but a very pretty one.

Mopsa. Let's have some merry ones.

Autolycus. Why, this is a passing merry one, and goes
to the tune of 'Two maids wooing a man': there's scarce
a maid westward but she sings it; 'tis in request, I can
tell you.

Mopsa. We can both sing it; if thou'lt bear a part, thou
shalt hear—'tis in three parts.   290

Dorcas. We had the tune on't a month ago.

Autolycus. I can bear my part—you must know 'tis my
occupation: have at it with you.

SONG

> *Autolycus.* Get you hence, for I must go
> Where it fits not you to know.
>   *Dorcas.* Whither?
>   *Mopsa.* O, whither?
>   *Dorcas.* Whither?
> *Mopsa.* It becomes thy oath full well,
> Thou to me thy secrets tell.   300
>   *Dorcas.* Me too: let me go thither.

Mopsa. Or thou goest to th' grange or mill.
Dorcas. If to either, thou dost ill.
Autolycus. Neither.
Dorcas. What, neither?
Autolycus. Neither.
Dorcas. Thou hast sworn my love to be.
Mopsa. Thou hast sworn it more to me.
       Then, whither goest? say, whither?

310   *Clown.* We'll have this song out anon by ourselves: my
father and the gentlemen are in sad talk, and we'll not
trouble them...Come, bring away thy pack after me.
Wenches, I'll buy for you both: pedlar, let's have the
first choice: follow me, girls.   [*they go out*
(*Autolycus.* And you shall pay well for 'em.
                         [*he goes out after them, singing*

       Will you buy any tape, or lace for your cape,
             My dainty duck, my dear-a?
       Any silk, any thread, any toys for your head,
             Of the new'st, and fin'st, fin'st wear-a?
320   Come to the pedlar, money's a meddler,
       That doth utter all men's ware-a.

                 The servant enters again

Servant. Master, there is three carters, three shepherds,
three neat-herds, three swine-herds, that have made
themselves all men of hair, they call themselves Saltiers,
and they have a dance which the wenches say is a gallimaufry of gambols, because they are not in't: but they
themselves are o'th' mind (if it be not too rough for some
that know little but bowling) it will please plentifully.

       Shepherd. Away! we'll none on't; here has been too
330 much homely foolery already....I know, sir, we weary
you.

Polixenes. You weary those that refresh us: pray, let's
see these four threes of herdsmen.

Servant. One three of them, by their own report, sir,
hath danced before the king; and not the worst of the
three but jumps twelve foot and a half by th squier.

Shepherd. Leave your prating—since these good men
are pleased, let them come in; but quickly now.

Servant. Why, they stay at door, sir.

[*he lets the herdsmen in*

'*Here a dance of twelve Satyrs*'

Polixenes. O, father, you'll know more of that here-
after...   340
[*to Camillo*] Is it not too far gone?'Tis time to part them—
He's simple, and tells much....[*to Florizel*] How now,
fair shepherd!
Your heart is full of something that does take
Your mind from feasting. Sooth, when I was young
And handed love as you do, I was wont
To load my She with knacks: I would have ransacked
The pedlar's silken treasury, and have poured it
To her acceptance; you have let him go,
And nothing marted with him. If your lass
Interpretation should abuse, and call this   350
Your lack of love or bounty, you were straited
For a reply, at least if you make a care
Of happy holding her.
Florizel.   Old sir, I know
She prizes not such trifles as these are:
The gifts she looks from me are packed and locked
Up in my heart, which I have given already,
But not delivered....O, hear me breathe my life
Before this ancient sir, who, it should seem,
Hath sometime loved: I take thy hand, this hand,

360 As soft as dove's down and as white as it,
    Or Ethiopian's tooth, or the fanned snow that's bolted
    By th' northern blasts twice o'er.
    Polixenes.   -   What follows this?
    How prettily th' young swain seems to wash
    The hand was fair before! I have put you out—
    But to your protestation; let me hear
    What you profess.
    Florizel.   Do, and be witness to't.
    Polixenes. And this my neighbour too?
    Florizel.   And he, and more
    Than he, and men, the earth, the heavens, and all...
    That, were I crowned the most imperial monarch,
370 Thereof most worthy; were I the fairest youth
    That ever made eye swerve, had force and knowledge
    More than was ever man's—I would not prize them,
    Without her love: for her, employ them all,
    Commend them and condemn them to her service
    Or to their own perdition.
    Polixenes.   Fairly offered.
    Camillo. This shows a sound affection.
    Shepherd.   But, my daughter,
    Say you the like to him?
    Perdita.   I cannot speak
    So well (nothing so well), no, nor mean better:
    By th' pattern of mine own thoughts I cut out
380 The purity of his.
    Shepherd.   Take hands, a bargain...
    And, friends unknown, you shall bear witness to't:
    I give my daughter to him, and will make
    Her portion equal his.
    Florizel.   O, that must be
    I'th' virtue of your daughter; one being dead,
    I shall have more than you can dream of yet,

Enough then for your wonder...But, come on,
Contract us 'fore these witnesses.

Shepherd. Come, your hand;
And, daughter, yours.

Polixenes. Soft, swain, awhile, beseech you—
Have you a father?

Florizel. I have: but what of him?

Polixenes. Knows he of this?

Florizel. He neither does nor shall. 390

Polixenes. Methinks, a father
Is at the nuptial of his son a guest
That best becomes the table...Pray you once more,
Is not your father grown incapable
Of reasonable affairs? is he not stupid
With age and alt'ring rheums? can he speak? hear?
Know man from man? dispute his own estate?
Lies he not bed-rid? and again does nothing,
But what he did being childish?

Florizel. No, good sir;
He has his health, and ampler strength indeed 400
Than most have of his age.

Polixenes. By my white beard,
You offer him, if this be so, a wrong
Something unfilial: reason my son
Should choose himself a wife, but as good reason
The father (all whose joy is nothing else
But fair posterity) should hold some counsel
In such a business.

Florizel. I yield all this;
But for some other reasons, my grave sir,
Which 'tis not fit you know, I not acquaint
My father of this business.

Polixenes. Let him know't. 410

Florizel. He shall not.

Polixenes.   Prithee, let him.

Florizel.   No, he must not.

Shepherd. Let him, my son, he shall not need to grieve
At knowing of thy choice.

Florizel.   Come, come he must not:
Mark our contract.

    Polixenes [*discovers himself*]. Mark your divorce,
       young sir,
Whom son I dare not call; thou art too base
To be acknowledged....Thou a sceptre's heir,
That thus affects a sheep-hook! Thou, old traitor,
I am sorry, that by hanging thee, I can
But shorten thy life one week....And thou, fresh piece
420 Of excellent witchcraft, who, of force, must know
The royal fool thou cop'st with—

    Shepherd.   O, my heart!

    Polixenes. I'll have thy beauty scratched with briars,
       and made
More homely than thy state....For thee, fond boy,
If I may ever know thou dost but sigh
That thou no more shalt see this knack (as never
I mean thou shalt) we'll bar thee from succession,
Not hold thee of our blood, no not our kin,
Farre than Deucalion off: mark thou my words!
Follow us to the court....Thou churl, for this time
430 (Though full of our displeasure) yet we free thee
From the dead blow of it....And you, enchantment—
Worthy enough a herdsman; yea, him too,
That makes himself (but for our honour therein)
Unworthy thee—if ever henceforth thou
These rural latches to his entrance open,
Or hoop his body more with thy embraces,
I will devise a death as cruel for thee,
As thou art tender to't.   [*he goes*

Perdita.   Even here, undone,
I was not much afeard: for once or twice
I was about to speak and tell him plainly,   440
The selfsame sun that shines upon his court
Hides not his visage from our cottage, but
Looks on alike....[*to Florizel*] Will't please you, sir, be
      gone?
I told you what would come of this: beseech you,
Of your own state take care: this dream of mine—
Being now awake, I'll queen it no inch farther,
But milk my ewes, and weep. [*she puts off her garland*
Camillo.   Why, how now, father!
Speak ere thou diest.
Shepherd.   I cannot speak, nor think,
Nor dare to know that which I know....[*to Florizel*] O, sir.
You have undone a man of fourscore three,   450
That thought to fill his grave in quiet; yea,
To die upon the bed my father died,
To lie close by his honest bones: but now
Some hangman must put on my shroud, and lay me
Where no priest shovels-in dust....[*to Perdita*] O curséd
      wretch!
That knew'st this was the prince, and wouldst adventure
To mingle faith with him....Undone! undone!
If I might die within this hour, I have lived
To die when I desire.
Florizel.   Why look you so upon me?
I am but sorry, not afeard; delayed,   460
But nothing alt'red: what I was, I am:
More straining on for plucking back; not following
My leash unwillingly.
Camillo.   Gracious my lord,
You know your father's temper: at this time
He will allow no speech...which, I do guess,

You do not purpose to him...and as hardly
Will he endure your sight as yet, I fear:
Then, till the fury of his highness settle,
Come not before him.

    Florizel.   I not purpose it...

470 I think, Camillo?

    Camillo.   Even he, my lord.

    Perdita. How often have I told you 'twould be thus?
How often said, my dignity would last
But till 'twere known?

    Florizel.   It cannot fail but by
The violation of my faith, and then
Let nature crush the sides o'th'earth together,
And mar the seeds within! Lift up thy looks:
From my succession wipe me, father, I
Am heir to my affection.

    Camillo.   Be advised.

    Florizel. I am; and by my fancy: if my reason
480 Will thereto be obedient, I have reason;
If not, my senses, better pleased with madness,
Do bid it welcome.

    Camillo.   This is desperate, sir.

    Florizel. So call it: but it does fulfil my vow;
I needs must think it honesty....Camillo,
Not for Bohemia, nor the pomp that may
Be thereat gleaned; for all the sun sees, or
The close earth wombs, or the profound seas hide
In unknown fathoms, will I break my oath
To this my fair beloved: therefore, I pray you,
490 As you have ever been my father's honoured friend
When he shall miss me (as, in faith, I mean not
To see him any more) cast your good counsels
Upon his passion; let myself and Fortune
Tug for the time to come....This you may know

And so deliver, I am put to sea
With her whom here I cannot hold on shore;
And most opportune to our need I have
A vessel rides fast by, but not prepared
For this design....What course I mean to hold
Shall nothing benefit your knowledge, nor   500
Concern me the reporting.
   Camillo.   O my lord,
I would your spirit were easier for advice,
Or stronger for your need.
   Florizel.   Hark, Perdita! [*he draws her aside*
[*to Camillo*] I'll hear you by and by.
   Camillo.   He's irremoveable,
Resolved for flight...Now were I happy, if
His going I could frame to serve my turn,
Save him from danger, do him love and honour,
Purchase the sight again of dear Sicilia,
And that unhappy king, my master, whom
I so much thirst to see.
   Florizel.   Now, good Camillo,   510
I am so fraught with curious business, that
I leave out ceremony.   [*he turns to go*
   Camillo.   Sir, I think
You have heard of my poor services i'th' love
That I have borne your father?
   Florizel.   Very nobly
Have you deserved: it is my father's music
To speak your deeds; not little of his care
To have them recompensed as thought on.
   Camillo.   Well, my lord,
If you may please to think I love the king,
And through him what is nearest to him, which is
Your gracious self, embrace but my direction,   520
If your more ponderous and settled project

May suffer alteration. On mine honour
I'll point you where you shall have such receiving
As shall become your highness, where you may
Enjoy your mistress; from the whom, I see,
There's no disjunction to be made, but by
(As heavens forfend!) your ruin; marry her;
And—with my best endeavours in your absence—
Your discontenting father strive to qualify,
530 And bring him up to liking.
    Florizel.   How, Camillo,
May this (almost a miracle) be done?
That I may call thee something more than man,
And after that trust to thee.
    Camillo.   Have you thought on
A place whereto you'll go?
    Florizel.   Not any yet:
But as th'unthought-on accident is guilty
To what we wildly do, so we profess
Ourselves to be the slaves of chance, and flies
Of every wind that blows.
    Camillo.   Then list to me:
This follows, if you will not change your purpose,
540 But undergo this flight; make for Sicilia,
And there present yourself and your fair princess,
(For so I see she must be) 'fore Leontes:
She shall be habited, as it becomes
The partner of your bed....Methinks I see
Leontes opening his free arms and weeping
His welcomes forth: asks thee, the son, forgiveness,
As 'twere i'th' father's person: kisses the hands
Of your fresh princess: o'er and o'er divides him
'Twixt his unkindness and his kindness; th'one
550 He chides to hell and bids the other grow
Faster than thought or time.

Florizel.   Worthy Camillo,
What colour for my visitation shall I
Hold up before him?
  Camillo.   Sent by the king your father
To greet him, and to give him comforts. Sir,
The manner of your bearing towards him, with
What you (as from your father) shall deliver,
Things known betwixt us three, I'll write you down,
The which shall point you forth at every sitting
What you must say; that he shall not perceive,
But that you have your father's bosom there,   560
And speak his very heart.
  Florizel.   I am bound to you:
There is some sap in this.
  Camillo.   A course more promising
Than a wild dedication of yourselves
To unpathed waters, undreamed shores; most certain,
To miseries enough: no hope to help you,
But as you shake off one to take another:
Nothing so certain as your anchors, who
Do their best office, if they can but stay you
Where you'll be loath to be: besides you know
Prosperity's the very bond of love,   570
Whose fresh complexion and whose heart together
Affliction alters.
  Perdita.   One of these is true:
I think affliction may subdue the cheek,
But not take in the mind.
  Camillo.   Yea? say you so?
[*to Florizel*] There shall not at your father's house these
     seven years
Be born another such.
  Florizel.   My good Camillo,
She is as forward of her breeding as

She is i'th' rear 'our birth.

   Camillo.   I cannot say 'tis pity

She lacks instructions, for she seems a mistress

580 To most that teach.

   Perdita.   Your pardon, sir. For this

I'll blush you thanks.

   Florizel.   My prettiest Perdita....[*he kisses her*

But, O, the thorns we stand upon! Camillo—

Preserver of my father, now of me,

The medicine of our house...how shall we do?

We are not furnished like Bohemia's son,

Nor shall appear in Sicilia.

   Camillo.   My lord,

Fear none of this: I think you know my fortunes

Do all lie there: it shall be so my care

To have you royally appointed, as if

590 The scene you play, were mine. For instance, sir,

That you may know you shall not want...one word.

                    [*they draw apart to the chimney-corner*

AUTOLYCUS enters and, supposing the room empty,
speaks his mind

   Autolycus. Ha, ha! what a fool Honesty is! and Trust,
his sworn brother, a very simple gentleman! I have sold
all my trumpery: not a counterfeit stone, not a ribbon,
glass, pomander, brooch, table-book, ballad, knife, tape,
glove, shoe-tie, bracelet, horn-ring, to keep my pack from
fasting: they throng who should buy first, as if my trin-
kets had been hallowed, and brought a benediction to the
buyer: by which means I saw whose purse was best in
600 picture; and, what I saw, to my good use I remembered.
My clown (who wants but something to be a reasonable
man) grew so in love with the wenches' song, that he
would not stir his pettitoes till he had both tune and

words, which so drew the rest of the herd to me, that all
their other senses stuck in ears: you might have pinched
a placket, it was senseless; 'twas nothing to geld a cod-
piece of a purse; I would have filed keys off that hung
in chains: no hearing, no feeling, but my sir's song, and
admiring the nothing of it. So that, in this time of leth-
argy, I picked and cut most of their festival purses: and 610
had not the old man come in with a hubbub against his
daughter and the king's son, and scared my choughs from
the chaff, I had not left a purse alive in the whole army.

[*Camillo, Florizel, and Perdita come forward;*
Autolycus slinks hastily behind a large press

Camillo. Nay, but my letters, by this means being there
So soon as you arrive, shall clear that doubt.

Florizel. And those that you'll procure from King
      Leontes?

Camillo. Shall satisfy your father.

Perdita.   Happy be you!
All that you speak shows fair.

Camillo [*seeing Autolycus*].   Who have we here?
We'll make an instrument of this; omit
Nothing may give us aid.   620

(*Autolycus.* If they have overheard me now...why,
hanging!

Camillo [*drags him forth*]. How now, good fellow!
Why shak'st thou so? Fear not, man—here's no harm
intended to thee.

Autolycus. I am a poor fellow, sir.

Camillo. Why, be so still; here's nobody will steal that
from thee: yet for the outside of thy poverty, we must make
an exchange; therefore disease thee instantly (thou must
think there's a necessity in't) and change garments with this 630
gentleman: though the pennyworth, on his side, be the
worst. yet hold thee, there's some boot. [*gives him money*

Autolycus. I am a poor fellow, sir...[*aside*] I know ye well enough.

[*Florizel sets his hat upon the table and, unbuttoning his doublet, withdraws into the chimney-corner*

Camillo. Nay, prithee, dispatch: the gentleman is half flayed already.

Autolycus. Are you in earnest, sir? [*aside*] I smell the trick on't.

Florizel. Dispatch, I prithee.

640 *Autolycus.* Indeed, I have had earnest, but I cannot with conscience take it.

Camillo. Unbuckle, unbuckle!

[*Autolycus follows Florizel to the chimney-corner*

Fortunate mistress (let my prophecy
Come home to ye!) you must retire yourself
Into some covert: take your sweetheart's hat
And pluck it o'er your brows, muffle your face,
Dismantle you, and (as you can) disliken
The truth of your own seeming, that you may
(For I do fear eyes over) to shipboard
650 Get undescried.

Perdita.   I see the play so lies
That I must bear a part.

Camillo.   No remedy....
Have you done there?

[*Florizel comes forward in the rags of Autolycus*

Florizel.   Should I now meet my father,
He would not call me son. [*takes his hat from the table*

Camillo [*snatches it and gives it to Perdita*]. Nay, you
        shall have no hat....

Come, lady, come...[*to Autolycus*] Farewell, my friend.

Autolycus [*steps forth half-dressed and makes a mock-
        courtly bow*].   Adieu, sir.

Florizel. O Perdita! what have we twain forgot?

Pray you, a word.   [*they talk apart*
(*Camillo.* What I do next, shall be to tell the king
Of this escape and whither they are bound;
Wherein, my hope is, I shall so prevail,
To force him after: in whose company   660
I shall review Sicilia; for whose sight
I have a woman's longing.
  Florizel.   Fortune speed us!
Thus we set on, Camillo, to th' sea-side.
  Camillo. The swifter speed, the better.

        [*Florizel, Perdita, and Camillo go out; Autolycus
            comes forward, dressing and talking the while*
Autolycus. I understand the business, I hear it: to have
an open ear, a quick eye, and a nimble hand, is necessary
for a cut-purse; a good nose is requisite also, to smell out
work for th'other senses. I see this is the time that the
unjust man doth thrive. What an exchange had this been,
without boot! [*strikes his leg*] What a boot is here, with 670
this exchange! Sure, the gods do this year connive at us,
and we may do any thing extempore. The prince himself
is about a piece of iniquity, stealing away from his father,
with his clog at his heels: if I thought it were a piece of
honesty to acquaint the king withal, I would not do't:
I hold it the more knavery to conceal it; and therein am
I constant to my profession.

        The CLOWN *and* SHEPHERD *enter*

Aside, aside! here is more matter for a hot brain: every
lane's end, every shop, church, session, hanging, yields
a careful man work.   [*he returns to the chimney-corner* 680
  Clown. See, see; what a man you are now! there is no
other way but to tell the king she's a changeling and none
of your flesh and blood.
  Shepherd. Nay, but hear me.

Clown. Nay, but hear me.

Shepherd. Go to then.

Clown. She being none of your flesh and blood, your flesh and blood has not offended the king, and so your flesh and blood is not to be punished by him. Show those
690 things you found about her—those secret things, all but what she has with her: this being done, let the law go whistle; I warrant you.

Shepherd. I will tell the king all, every word, yea, and his son's pranks too; who, I may say, is no honest man, neither to his father nor to me, to go about to make me the king's brother-in-law.

Clown. Indeed, brother-in-law was the farthest off you could have been to him, and then your blood had been the dearer by I know not how much an ounce.

700 (*Autolycus.* Very wisely—puppies!

Shepherd. Well; let us to the king...[*takes a bundle from the press*] There is that in this fardel will make him scratch his beard.

(*Autolycus.* I know not what impediment this complaint may be to the flight of my master.

Clown. Pray heartily he be at' palace.

(*Autolycus.* Though I am not naturally honest, I am so sometimes by chance: let me pocket up my pedlar's excrement....[*takes off his false beard and steps forth*] How
710 now, rustics? whither are you bound?

Shepherd. To th' palace, an it like your worship.

Autolycus. Your affairs there? what? with whom? the condition of that fardel, the place of your dwelling, your names, your ages, of what having, breeding, and any thing that is fitting to be known, discover.

Clown. We are but plain fellows, sir.

Autolycus. A lie; you are rough and hairy: let me have no lying; it becomes none but tradesmen, and they often

give us soldiers the lie, but we pay them for it with
stamped coin, not stabbing steel, therefore they do not 720
give us the lie.

Clown. Your worship had like to have given us one, if
you had not taken yourself with the manner.

Shepherd. Are you a courtier, an't like you, sir?

Autolycus. Whether it like me or no, I am a courtier.
Seest thou not the air of the court in these enfoldings?
hath not my gait in it the measure of the court? receives
not thy nose court-odour from me? reflect I not on thy
baseness court-contempt? Think'st thou, for that I insinuate to toaze from thee thy business, I am therefore 730
no courtier? I am courtier cap-a-pe; and one that will
either push on or pluck back thy business there: whereupon I command thee to open thy affair.

Shepherd. My business, sir, is to the king.

Autolycus. What advocate hast thou to him?

Shepherd. I know not, an't like you.

(*Clown.* Advocate's the court-word for a pheasant; say
you have none.

Shepherd. None, sir; I have no pheasant, cock nor hen.

Autolycus. How blessed are we that are not simple men! 740
Yet nature might have made me as these are,
Therefore I will not disdain.

Clown. This cannot but be a great courtier!

Shepherd. His garments are rich, but he wears them
not handsomely.

Clown. He seems to be the more noble in being fan-
tastical: a great man, I'll warrant; I know by the picking
on's teeth.

Autolycus. The fardel there? what's i'th' fardel? Where-
fore that box? 750

Shepherd. Sir, there lies such secrets in this fardel and
box, which none must know but the king, and which he

shall know within this hour, if I may come to th' speech of him.

Autolycus. Age, thou hast lost thy labour.

Shepherd. Why, sir?

Autolycus. The king is not at the palace, he is gone aboard a new ship to purge melancholy and air himself: for, if thou beest capable of things serious, thou must 760 know the king is full of grief.

Shepherd. So 'tis said, sir; about his son, that should have married a shepherd's daughter.

Autolycus. If that shepherd be not in hand-fast, let him fly; the curses he shall have, the tortures he shall feel, will break the back of man, the heart of monster.

Clown. Think you so, sir?

Autolycus. Not he alone shall suffer what wit can make heavy and vengeance bitter; but those that are germane to him, though removed fifty times, shall all come under 770 the hangman: which though it be great pity, yet it is necessary. An old sheep-whistling rogue, a ram-tender, to offer to have his daughter come into grace! Some say he shall be stoned; but that death is too soft for him, say I: draw our throne into a sheep-cote! all deaths are too few, the sharpest too easy.

Clown. Has the old man e'er a son, sir, do you hear, an't like you, sir?

Autolycus. He has a son...who shall be flayed alive, then 'nointed over with honey, set on the head of a wasp's 780 nest, then stand till he be three quarters and a dram dead; then recovered again with aqua-vitæ or some other hot infusion; then, raw as he is, and in the hottest day prognostication proclaims, shall he be set against a brick-wall, the sun looking with a southward eye upon him; where he is to behold him with flies blown to death. But what talk we of these traitorly rascals, whose miseries are to be smiled at, their offences being so capital? Tell me (for you seem to be honest plain men) what you have to the king: being something gently considered, I'll bring you where he is aboard, tender your persons to his presence, 790 whisper him in your behalfs; and, if it be in man, besides the king, to effect your suits, here is man shall do it.

(Clown. He seems to be of great authority: close with him, give him gold; and though authority be a stubborn bear, yet he is oft led by the nose with gold: show the inside of your purse to the outside of his hand, and no more ado. Remember 'stoned,' and 'flayed alive!'

Shepherd. An't please you, sir, to undertake the business for us, here is that gold I have: I'll make it as much more, and leave this young man in pawn, till I bring it you. 800

Autolycus. After I have done what I promised?

Shepherd. Ay, sir.

Autolycus. Well, give me the moiety...Are you a party in this business?

Clown. In some sort, sir: but though my case be a pitiful one, I hope I shall not be flayed out of it.

Autolycus. O, that's the case of the shepherd's son: hang him, he'll be made an example.

(Clown. Comfort, good comfort! We must to the king, and show our strange sights: he must know 'tis none of 810 your daughter nor my sister; we are gone else....[to Autolycus] Sir, I will give you as much as this old man does, when the business is performed, and remain, as he says, your pawn till it be brought you.

Autolycus. I will trust you. Walk before toward the sea-side, go on the right hand, I will but look upon the hedge and follow you.

Clown. We are blest in this man, as I may say, even blest.

Shepherd. Let's before, as he bids us: he was provided to do us good. [Shepherd and Clown go out 820

Autolycus. If I had a mind to be honest, I see Fortune would not suffer me; she drops booties in my mouth. I am courted now with a double occasion: gold and a means to do the prince my master good; which who knows how that may turn back to my advancement? I will bring these two moles, these blind ones, aboard him: if he think it fit to shore them again, and that the complaint they have to the king concerns him nothing, let him call me rogue for being so far officious, for I am
830 proof against that title and what shame else belongs to't...To him will I present them, there may be matter in it.   [*he goes*

[5. 1.] *Sicilia. A room in the palace of Leontes*

LEONTES, CLEOMENES, DION, PAULINA, *and others*

Cleomenes. Sir, you have done enough, and have performed
A saint-like sorrow: no fault could you make,
Which you have not redeemed; indeed, paid down
More penitence than done trespass: at the last,
Do as the heavens have done, forget your evil;
With them forgive yourself.
    Leontes.   Whilst I remember
Her and her virtues, I cannot forget
My blemishes in them, and so still think of
The wrong I did myself: which was so much,
10 That heirless it hath made my kingdom, and
Destroyed the sweet'st companion that e'er man
Bred his hopes out of.
    Paulina.   True, too true, my lord:
If, one by one, you wedded all the world,
Or from the all that are took something good

To make a perfect woman...she you killed
Would be unparalleled.
  Leontes.　　　　　　　I think so....Killed!
She I killed! I did so: but thou strik'st me
Sorely, to say I did; it is as bitter
Upon thy tongue, as in my thought....Now, good now,
Say so but seldom.
  Cleomenes.　　　　Not at all, good lady:　　　　　20
You might have spoken a thousand things that would
Have done the time more benefit and graced
Your kindness better.
  Paulina.　　　　　　You are one of those
Would have him wed again.
  Dion.　　　　　　　　If you would not so,
You pity not the state, nor the remembrance
Of his most sovereign name; consider little
What dangers, by his highness' fail of issue,
May drop upon his kingdom, and devour
Incertain lookers on. What were more holy
Than to rejoice the former queen is well?　　　　30
What holier than, for royalty's repair,
For present comfort and for future good,
To bless the bed of majesty again
With a sweet fellow to't?
  Paulina.　　　　　There is none worthy,
Respecting her that's gone...Besides, the gods
Will have fulfilled their secret purposes:
For has not the divine Apollo said,
Is't not the tenour of his oracle,
That King Leontes shall not have an heir
Till his lost child be found? which, that it shall,　　40
Is all as monstrous to our human reason,
As my Antigonus to break his grave,
And come again to me; who, on my life,

Did perish with the infant. 'Tis your counsel
My lord should to the heavens be contrary,
Oppose against their wills....[*to Leontes*] Care not for
    issue—
The crown will find an heir: great Alexander
Left his to th' worthiest; so his successor
Was like to be the best.
    Leontes.   Good Paulina,
50 Who hast the memory of Hermione
I know in honour...O, that ever I
Had squared me to thy counsel! then, even now,
I might have looked upon my queen's full eyes,
Have taken treasure from her lips—
    Paulina.   And left them
More rich for what they yielded.
    Leontes.   Thou speak'st truth:
No more such wives, therefore no wife: one worse,
And better used, would make her sainted spirit
Again possess her corpse, and on this stage,
† Where we offenders move, appear soul-vexed,
60 And begin, 'Why to me?'
    Paulina.   Had she such power,
She had just cause.
    Leontes.   She had, and would incense me
To murder her I married.
    Paulina.   I should so:
Were I the ghost that walked, I'ld bid you mark
Her eye, and tell me for what dull part in't
You chose her: then I'ld shriek, that even your ears
Should rift to hear me, and the words that followed
Should be, 'Remember mine!'
    Leontes.   Stars, stars,
And all eyes else dead coals! Fear thou no wife;
I'll have no wife, Paulina.

Paulina. Will you swear
Never to marry, but by my free leave? 70
  Leontes. Never, Paulina, so be blest my spirit!
  Paulina. Then, good my lords, bear witness to his oath.
  Cleomenes. You tempt him over-much.
  Paulina. Unless another,
As like Hermione as is her picture,
Affront his eye.
  Cleomenes. Good madam,—
  Paulina. I have done.
Yet, if my lord will marry...if you will, sir...
No remedy, but you will...give me the office
To choose you a queen: she shall not be so young
As was your former, but she shall be such
As, walked your first queen's ghost, it should take joy 80
To see her in your arms.
  Leontes. My true Paulina,
We shall not marry, till thou bid'st us.
  Paulina. That
Shall be when your first queen's again in breath;
Never till then.

A gentleman enters

  Gentleman. One that gives out himself Prince Florizel,
Son of Polixenes, with his princess (she
The fairest I have yet beheld) desires access
To your high presence.
  Leontes. What with him? he comes not
Like to his father's greatness: his approach
(So out of circumstance and sudden) tells us 90
'Tis not a visitation framed, but forced
By need and accident. What train?
  Gentleman. But few,
And those but mean.

Leontes.   His princess, say you, with him?

Gentleman. Ay; the most peerless piece of earth, I
    think,
That e'er the sun shone bright on.

Paulina.   O Hermione,
As every present time doth boast itself
Above a better gone, so must thy grave
Give way to what's seen now! Sir, you yourself
Have said and writ so; but your writing now
100 Is colder than that theme: 'She had not been,
Nor was not to be equalled'—thus your verse
Flowed with her beauty once; 'tis shrewdly ebbed,
To say you have seen a better.

Gentleman.   Pardon, madam:
The one I have almost forgot—your pardon—
The other, when she has obtained your eye,
Will have your tongue too. This is a creature,
Would she begin a sect, might quench the zeal
Of all professors else; make proselytes
Of who she but bid follow.

Paulina.   How! not women?

110 *Gentleman.* Women will love her, that she is a woman
More worth than any man; men, that she is
The rarest of all women.

Leontes.   Go, Cleomenes,
Yourself, assisted with your honoured friends,
Bring them to our embracement....

                    [*Cleomenes and others hurry forth*
                         Still, 'tis strange,
He thus should steal upon us.

Paulina.   Had our prince
(Jewel of children) seen this hour, he had paired
Well with this lord; there was not full a month
Between their births.

Leontes. Prithee, no more; cease; thou know'st,
He dies to me again when talked of: sure,   120
When I shall see this gentleman, thy speeches
Will bring me to consider that which may
Unfurnish me of reason.   They are come.

CLEOMENES *returns with* FLORIZEL, PERDITA,
and attendants

Your mother was most true to wedlock, prince,
For she did print your royal father off,
Conceiving you: were I but twenty-one,
Your father's image is so hit in you
(His very air!) that I should call you brother,
As I did him, and speak of something wildly
By us performed before. Most dearly welcome!   130
And your fair princess [*she unveils*]—goddess! O!
      [*he gazes at her*]...Alas,
I lost a couple, that 'twixt heaven and earth
Might thus have stood begetting wonder, as
You, gracious couple, do: and then I lost
(All mine own folly) the society,
Amity too, of your brave father, whom
(Though bearing misery) I desire my life
Once more to look on him.
    Florizel.   By his command
Have I here touched Sicilia, and from him
Give you all greetings, that a king, at friend,   140
Can send his brother: and, but infirmity,
Which waits upon worn times, hath something seized
His wished ability, he had himself
The lands and waters 'twixt your throne and his
Measured to look upon you; whom he loves
(He bade me say so) more than all the sceptres,
And those that bear them, living.

7   PSWT

Leontes.   O my brother
(Good gentleman!) the wrongs I have done thee stir
Afresh within me; and these thy offices,
150 So rarely kind, are as interpreters
Of my behind-hand slackness....Welcome hither,
As is the spring to th'earth. And hath he too
Exposed this paragon to th' fearful usage
(At least ungentle) of the dreadful Neptune,
To greet a man not worth her pains, much less
Th'adventure of her person?
   Florizel.   Good my lord,
She came from Libya.
   Leontes.   Where the warlike Smalus,
That noble honoured lord, is feared and loved?
   Florizel. Most royal sir, from thence; from him, whose
       daughter
160 His tears proclaimed his, parting with her: thence
(A prosperous south-wind friendly) we have crossed,
To execute the charge my father gave me,
For visiting your highness: my best train
I have from your Sicilian shores dismissed;
Who for Bohemia bend, to signify
Not only my success in Libya, sir,
But my arrival, and my wife's, in safety
Here, where we are.
   Leontes.   The blessed gods
Purge all infection from our air, whilst you
170 Do climate here! You have a holy father,
A graceful gentleman, against whose person
(So sacred as it is) I have done sin,
For which the heavens, taking angry note,
Have left me issueless; and your father's blessed
(As he from heaven merits it) with you,
Worthy his goodness....What might I have been,

Might I a son and daughter now have looked on,
Such goodly things as you?

A lord enters

Lord.   Most noble sir,
That which I shall report will bear no credit,
Were not the proof so nigh. Please you, great sir,   180
Bohemia greets you from himself, by me:
Desires you to attach his son, who has
(His dignity and duty both cast off)
Fled from his father, from his hopes, and with
A shepherd's daughter.
    Leontes.   Where's Bohemia? speak!
    Lord. Here in your city; I now came from him.
I speak amazedly, and it becomes
My marvel and my message. To your court
Whiles he was hast'ning (in the chase, it seems,
Of this fair couple) meets he on the way   190
The father of this seeming lady, and
Her brother, having both their country quitted
With this young prince.
    Florizel.   Camillo has betrayed me;
Whose honour and whose honesty till now
Endured all weathers.
    Lord.   Lay't so to his charge:
He's with the king your father.
    Leontes.   Who? Camillo?
    Lord. Camillo, sir; I spake with him; who now
Has these poor men in question. Never saw I
Wretches so quake: they kneel, they kiss the earth;
Forswear themselves as often as they speak: 200
Bohemia stops his ears, and threatens them
With divers deaths in death.
    Perdita.   O, my poor father!

The heaven sets spies upon us, will not have
Our contract celebrated.
   Leontes.   You are married?
   Florizel. We are not, sir, nor are we like to be;
The stars, I see, will kiss the valleys first:
The odds for high and low's alike.
   Leontes.   My lord,
Is this the daughter of a king?
   Florizel.   She is,
When once she is my wife.
210 *Leontes.* That 'once,' I see, by your good father's speed,
Will come on very slowly. I am sorry
(Most sorry) you have broken from his liking,
Where you were tied in duty: and as sorry,
Your choice is not so rich in worth as beauty,
That you might well enjoy her.
   Florizel.   Dear, look up:
Though Fortune, visible an enemy,
Should chase us with my father; power no jot
Hath she to change our loves....[*kneels*] Beseech you, sir,
Remember since you owed no more to time
220 Than I do now: with thought of such affections,
Step forth mine advocate; at your request,
My father will grant precious things as trifles.
   Leontes. Would he do so, I'ld beg your precious mis-
       tress,
Which he counts but a trifle.
   Paulina.   Sir, my liege,
Your eye hath too much youth in't: not a month
'Fore your queen died, she was more worth such gazes
Than what you look on now.
   Leontes.   I thought of her,
Even in these looks I made....[*to Florizel*] But your
       petition

Is yet unanswered: I will to your father:
Your honour not o'erthrown by your desires,   230
I am friend to them and you: upon which errand
I now go toward him; therefore follow me,
And mark what way I make: come, good my lord.

                                              [*they go*

[5. 2.]   *Before the palace of Leontes*

              AUTOLYCUS *and a gentleman*

Autolycus. Beseech you, sir, were you present at this
relation?

1 *Gentleman.* I was by at the opening of the fardel,
heard the old shepherd deliver the manner how he found
it: whereupon, after a little amazedness, we were all
commanded out of the chamber; only this methought I
heard the shepherd say, he found the child.

Autolycus. I would most gladly know the issue of it.

1 *Gentleman.* I make a broken delivery of the business:
but the changes I perceived in the king and Camillo 10
were very notes of admiration: they seemed almost, with
staring on one another, to tear the cases of their eyes;
there was speech in their dumbness, language in their
very gesture; they looked as they had heard of a world
ransomed, or one destroyed: a notable passion of wonder
appeared in them: but the wisest beholder, that knew no
more but seeing, could not say if th'importance were joy
or sorrow; but in the extremity of the one, it must needs
be.

           Another gentleman comes up

Here comes a gentleman, that haply knows more: the 20
news, Rogero?

2 *Gentleman.* Nothing but bonfires: the oracle is ful-

filled; the king's daughter is found: such a deal of wonder
is broken out within this hour, that ballad-makers cannot
be able to express it.

A third gentleman approaches

Here comes the Lady Paulina's steward, he can deliver
you more. How goes it now, sir? this news which is
called true is so like an old tale, that the verity of it is in
strong suspicion: has the king found his heir?

30 3 *Gentleman*. Most true, if ever Truth were pregnant
by Circumstance: that which you hear you'll swear you
see, there is such unity in the proofs. The mantle of
Queen Hermione's: her jewel about the neck of it: the
letters of Antigonus found with it, which they know to be
his character: the majesty of the creature, in resemblance
of the mother: the affection of nobleness, which nature
shows above her breeding—and many other evidences,
proclaim her, with all certainty, to be the king's daughter.
Did you see the meeting of the two kings?

40 2 *Gentleman*. No.

3 *Gentleman*. Then have you lost a sight, which was to
be seen, cannot be spoken of. There might you have beheld one joy crown another, so and in such manner, that
it seemed sorrow wept to take leave of them; for their joy
waded in tears. There was casting up of eyes, holding up
of hands, with countenance of such distraction, that they
were to be known by garment, not by favour. Our king
being ready to leap out of himself for joy of his found
daughter; as if that joy were now become a loss, cries,
50 'O, thy mother, thy mother!' then asks Bohemia forgiveness, then embraces his son-in-law; then again worries
he his daughter, with clipping her; now he thanks the
old shepherd, which stands by, like a weather-bitten conduit of many kings' reigns. I never heard of such another

encounter, which lames report to follow it, and undoes description to do it.

2 *Gentleman.* What, pray you, became of Antigonus, that carried hence the child?

3 *Gentleman.* Like an old tale still, which will have matter to rehearse, though credit be asleep and not an 60 ear open; he was torn to pieces with a bear: this avouches the shepherd's son; who has not only his innocence (which seems much) to justify him, but a handkerchief and rings of his that Paulina knows.

1 *Gentleman.* What became of his bark and his followers?

3 *Gentleman.* Wracked the same instant of their master's death, and in the view of the shepherd: so that all the instruments which aided to expose the child were even then lost, when it was found. But, O, the noble combat 70 that 'twixt joy and sorrow was fought in Paulina! She had one eye declined for the loss of her husband, another elevated that the oracle was fulfilled: she lifted the princess from the earth, and so locks her in embracing, as if she would pin her to her heart, that she might no more be in danger of losing.

1 *Gentleman.* The dignity of this act was worth the audience of kings and princes, for by such was it acted.

3 *Gentleman.* One of the prettiest touches of all, and 80 that which angled for mine eyes (caught the water, though not the fish) was, when at the relation of the queen's death (with the manner how she came to't, bravely confessed and lamented by the king) how attentiveness wounded his daughter, till, from one sign of dolour to another, she did, with an 'Alas,' I would fain say, bleed tears; for, I am sure, my heart wept blood. Who was most marble, there changed colour; some

swooned, all sorrowed: if all the world could have seen't,
90 the woe had been universal.

1 *Gentleman.* Are they returned to the court?

3 *Gentleman.* No: the princess hearing of her mother's
statue, which is in the keeping of Paulina—a piece many
years in doing, and now newly performed, by that rare
Italian master, Julio Romano, who, had he himself
eternity and could put breath into his work, would be-
guile nature of her custom, so perfectly he is her ape: he
so near to Hermione hath done Hermione, that they say
one would speak to her and stand in hope of answer.
100 Thither with all greediness of affection are they gone,
and there they intend to sup.

2 *Gentleman.* I thought she had some great matter
there in hand, for she hath privately twice or thrice a day,
ever since the death of Hermione, visited that removed
house. Shall we thither, and with our company piece the
rejoicing?

1 *Gentleman.* Who would be thence that has the benefit
of access? Every wink of an eye, some new grace will be
born: our absence makes us unthrifty to our knowledge.
110 Let's along. [*the three gentlemen go off, talking together*
Autolycus. Now, had I not the dash of my former life
in me, would preferment drop on my head. I brought
the old man and his son aboard the prince; told him I
heard them talk of a fardel and I know not what: but he
at that time, over-fond of the shepherd's daughter (so he
then took her to be) who began to be much sea-sick, and
himself little better, extremity of weather continuing, this
mystery remained undiscovered. But 'tis all one to me:
for had I been the finder out of this secret, it would not
120 have relished among my other discredits.

The SHEPHERD and CLOWN approach, in fine apparel

Here come those I have done good to against my will,
and already appearing in the blossoms of their fortune.

Shepherd. Come, boy; I am past moe children; but
thy sons and daughters will be all gentlemen born.

Clown. You are well met, sir. You denied to fight with
me this other day, because I was no gentleman born. See
you these clothes? Say you see them not and think me
still no gentleman born: you were best say these robes
are not gentlemen born. Give me the lie; do; and try
whether I am not now a gentleman born.   130

Autolycus. I know, you are now, sir, a gentleman born.

Clown. Ay, and have been so any time these four hours.

Shepherd. And so have I, boy.

Clown. So you have: but I was a gentleman born before my father: for the king's son took me by the hand,
and called me brother; and then the two kings called my
father brother; and then the prince, my brother, and the
princess, my sister, called my father father; and so we
wept: and there was the first gentleman-like tears that
ever we shed.   140

Shepherd. We may live, son, to shed many more.

Clown. Ay; or else 'twere hard luck, being in so pre-
posterous estate as we are.

Autolycus. I humbly beseech you, sir, to pardon me all
the faults I have committed to your worship, and to give
me your good report to the prince my master.

Shepherd. Prithee, son, do; for we must be gentle, now
we are gentlemen.

Clown. Thou wilt amend thy life?

Autolycus. Ay, an it like your good worship.   150

Clown. Give me thy hand: I will swear to the prince
thou art as honest a true fellow as any is in Bohemia.

Shepherd. You may say it, but not swear it.

Clown. Not swear it, now I am a gentleman? Let
boors and franklins say it, I'll swear it.

Shepherd. How if it be false, son?

Clown. If it be ne'er so false, a true gentleman may
swear it, in the behalf of his friend: and I'll swear to the
prince thou art a tall fellow of thy hands, and that thou
160 wilt not be drunk; but I know thou art no tall fellow of
thy hands and that thou wilt be drunk; but I'll swear it,
and I would thou wouldst be a tall fellow of thy hands.

Autolycus. I will prove so, sir, to my power.

Clown. Ay, by any means prove a tall fellow: if I do
not wonder how thou darest venture to be drunk, not
being a tall fellow, trust me not. Hark! the kings and
the princes, our kindred, are going to see the queen's
picture. Come, follow us: we'll be thy good masters.

[*they go*

[5. 3.]   *A chapel in Paulina's house: at the*
upper end a niche with a curtain before it

LEONTES, POLIXENES, FLORIZEL, PERDITA, CAMILLO,
and PAULINA *enter with lords and attendants*

Leontes. O grave and good Paulina, the great comfort
That I have had of thee!

Paulina.   What, sovereign sir,
I did not well, I meant well; all my services
You have paid home: but that you have vouchsafed,
With your crowned brother and these contracted
Heirs of your kingdoms, my poor house to visit,
It is a surplus of your grace, which never
My life may last to answer.

Leontes.   O Paulina,
We honour you with trouble: but we came

To see the statue of our queen: your gallery   10
Have we passed through, not without much content
In many singularities; but we saw not
That which my daughter came to look upon,
The statue of her mother.

 Paulina.   As she lived peerless,
So her dead likeness, I do well believe,
Excels whatever yet you looked upon,
Or hand of man hath done; therefore I keep it
Lonely, apart. But here it is: prepare
To see the life as lively mocked, as ever
Still sleep mocked death: behold, and say 'tis well....   20
 [*Paulina draws the curtain, and discovers the figure*
I like your silence, it the more shows off
Your wonder: but yet speak—first, you, my liege—
Comes it not something near?

 Leontes.   Her natural posture!
Chide me, dear stone, that I may say indeed
Thou art Hermione; or rather, thou art she
In thy not chiding; for she was as tender
As infancy and grace. But yet, Paulina,
Hermione was not so much wrinkled, nothing
So agéd as this seems.

 Polixenes.   O, not by much.

 Paulina. So much the more our carver's excellence,   30
Which lets go by some sixteen years, and makes her
As she lived now.

 Leontes.   As now she might have done,
So much to my good comfort, as it is
Now piercing to my soul. O, thus she stood,
Even with such life of majesty (warm life,
As now it coldly stands) when first I wooed her!
I am ashamed: does not the stone rebuke me,
For being more stone than it? O royal piece!

There's magic in thy majesty, which has
40 My evils conjured to remembrance, and
From thy admiring daughter took the spirits,
Standing like stone with thee!
    Perdita.   And give me leave,
And do not say 'tis superstition, that
I kneel and then implore her blessing....[*kneels*] Lady,
Dear queen, that ended when I but began,
Give me that hand of yours to kiss.
    Paulina [*prevents her*].   O, patience;
The statue is but newly fixed; the colour's
Not dry.
    Camillo. My lord, your sorrow was too sore laid on,
50 Which sixteen winters cannot blow away,
So many summers dry: scarce any joy
Did ever so long live; no sorrow,
But killed itself much sooner.
    Polixenes.   Dear my brother,
Let him that was the cause of this have power
To take off so much grief from you, as he
Will piece up in himself.
    Paulina.   Indeed, my lord,
If I had thought the sight of my poor image
Would thus have wrought you (for the stone is mine)
I'ld not have showed it.   [*she moves to the curtain*
    Leontes.   Do not draw the curtain.
60 *Paulina.* No longer shall you gaze on't, lest your fancy
May think anon it moves.
    Leontes.   Let be, let be!
Would I were dead, but that, methinks, already!—
What was he that did make it?—See, my lord,
Would you not deem it breathed? and that those veins
Did verily bear blood?
    Polixenes.   Masterly done:

The very life seems warm upon her lip.

Leontes. The fixure of her eye has motion in't,
As we are mocked with art.

Paulina.   I'll draw the curtain:
My lord's almost so far transported that
He'll think anon it lives.

Leontes.   O sweet Paulina,   70
Make me to think so twenty years together;
No settled senses of the world can match
The pleasure of that madness. Let't alone.

Paulina. I am sorry, sir, I have thus far stirred you: but
I could afflict you farther.

Leontes.   Do, Paulina;
For this affliction has a taste as sweet
As any cordial comfort. Still methinks
There is an air comes from her. What fine chisel
Could ever yet cut breath? Let no man mock me,
For I will kiss her.

Paulina.   Good my lord, forbear: 80
The ruddiness upon her lip is wet;
You'll mar it, if you kiss it; stain your own
With oily painting...Shall I draw the curtain?

Leontes. No! not these twenty years.

Perdita.   So long could I
Stand by, a looker on.

Paulina.   Either forbear,
Quit presently the chapel, or resolve you
For more amazement: if you can behold it,
I'll make the statue move indeed; descend,
And take you by the hand: but then you'll think
(Which I protest against) I am assisted   90
By wicked powers.

Leontes.   What you can make her do,
I am content to look on: what to speak,

I am content to hear; for 'tis as easy
To make her speak, as move.

    Paulina.   It is required
You do awake your faith: then all stand still;
Or those that think it is unlawful business
I am about, let them depart.

    Leontes.   Proceed:
No foot shall stir.

    Paulina.   Music; awake her: strike!   *[music*
'Tis time; descend; be stone no more; approach;
100 Strike all that look upon with marvel; come;
I'll fill your grave up; stir; nay, come away;
Bequeath to death your numbness, for from him
Dear life redeems you! You perceive, she stirs:
                 [Hermione comes down from the pedestal
Start not: her actions shall be holy, as
You hear my spell is lawful: do not shun her
Until you see her die again; for then
You kill her double: nay, present your hand:
When she was young, you wooed her; now, in age,
Is she become the suitor? *[Hermione embraces Leontes*

    Leontes.   O, she's warm!
110 If this be magic, let it be an art
Lawful as eating.   *[they kiss again*

    Polixenes.   She embraces him!

    Camillo. She hangs about his neck—
If she pertain to life, let her speak too.

    Polixenes. Ay, and make it manifest where she has
        lived,
Or how stol'n from the dead.

    Paulina.   That she is living,
Were it but told you, should be hooted at
Like an old tale; but it appears she lives,
Though yet she speak not. Mark a little while...

Please you to interpose, fair madam, kneel
And pray your mother's blessing....Turn, good lady, 120
Our Perdita is found.

           [she presents Perdita, who kneels once more
  Hermione.   You gods look down,
And from your sacred vials pour your graces
Upon my daughter's head! Tell me (mine own)
Where hast thou been preserved? where lived? how
    found
Thy father's court? for thou shalt hear that I,
Knowing by Paulina that the oracle
Gave hope thou wast in being, have preserved
Myself to see the issue.

  Paulina.   There's time enough for that,
Lest they desire (upon this push) to trouble
Your joys with like relation....Go together, 130
You precious winners all; your exultation
Partake to every one: I (an old turtle)
Will wing me to some withered bough, and there
My mate (that's never to be found again)
Lament, till I am lost.

  Leontes.   O peace, Paulina!
Thou shouldst a husband take by my consent,
As I by thine a wife: this is a match,
And made between's by vows. Thou hast found mine,
But how, is to be questioned: for I saw her,
As I thought, dead; and have, in vain, said many 140
A prayer upon her grave: I'll not seek far
(For him, I partly know his mind) to find thee
An honourable husband—come, Camillo,
And take her by the hand—whose worth and honesty
Is richly noted; and here justified
By us, a pair of kings....Let's from this place....
What? look upon my brother: both your pardons,

That e'er I put between your holy looks
My ill suspicion....This' your son-in-law,
150 And son unto the king, whom heavens directing,
Is troth-plight to your daughter. Good Paulina,
Lead us from hence, where we may leisurely
Each one demand and answer to his part
Performed in this wide gap of time, since first
We were dissevered: hastily lead away.   [*they go*

GLOSSARY

Note. Where a pun or quibble is intended, the meanings are distinguished as (*a*) and (*b*)

ABIDE, sojourn (for a while only); 4. 3. 90

ABILITY, strength; 2. 3. 164; 5. 1. 143

ACCOMPT (beyond), 'unprecedented' (Furness); 2. 3. 198

ADMIRATION (notes of), notes of exclamation; 5. 2. 11

AFFECTION, (i) lust; 1. 2. 138; (ii) natural disposition; 5. 2. 36

AFFRONT, confront (cf. *Ham.* 3. 1. 31 'That he...may here affront Ophelia'); 5. 1. 75

ALLOWING, approving, applauding (cf. Sidney, *Arcadia*, 'with many allowing tokens was Euarchus speech heard'); 1. 2. 185

ALTERING, i.e. changing the physical processes either (by disease) for the bad or (by medicine) for the good (cf. *N.E.D.* 'altering' 2, 'alterative,' and 'alteration' = distemper, quoting Burton, *Anat.* 'Strange meats...cause notable alterations and distempers'); 4. 4. 396

ANCIENTRY, old people (*N.E.D.* quotes *Plain Percevall*, 1589, 'the Auncientry of the Parish'); 3. 3. 62

ANGLE, hook; 4. 2. 45

ANSWER, lit. reply to a charge, hence—charge; 3. 2. 198

APE-BEARER, 'one who carries a monkey about for exhibition, a strolling buffoon' (*N.E.D.*); 4. 3. 92

APPOINT, ordain, devote (a person or thing to some fate), v. *N.E.D.* 'appoint' 11, quoting 1 *Thes.* v. 9 'God hath not appointed us to wrath'; 1. 2. 326

APPROBATION, proof; 2. 1. 177

APPROVE, prove; 4. 2. 27

ARGUMENT, theme; 4. 1. 29

ASPECT. Astrol. the position or appearance of the stars, etc., as viewed from the earth; 2. 1. 107

ATTACH, arrest; 5. 1. 182

ATTORNEY (vb.), perform at second-hand; 1. 1. 26

AVAIL, be profitable, be of use; 3. 2. 86

AVOID, quit; 1. 2. 462.

BAILIFF, 'an officer of justice under a sheriff, who executes writs and processes, distrains and arrests; a warrant officer, pursuivant or catchpoll' (*N.E.D.*); cf. *Errors*, G. 'sergeant of the band'; 4. 3. 93

BASILISK, or cockatrice, a fabulous reptile, half cock and half serpent, supposed to be able to kill by its breath or look; 1. 2. 388

BASTARD, i.e. not a pure natural breed but the product of an artificial crossing of different stocks; 4. 4. 83

BAWCOCK, fine fellow (Fr. 'beau coq'). A colloquial term of endearment; 1. 2. 121.

BEAR-BAITING. One of the most popular of English sports in Sh.'s day. The bear was tied by a long chain to a stake in the middle of a ring and was then set upon by a number of mastiffs (cf. *Sh Eng.* ii. 428 ff.); 4. 3. 99

BEARING-CLOTH, christening-robe; 3. 3. 110

BED-SWERVER, one unfaithful in marriage; 2. 1. 93

Bench (vb.), raise to official dignity (cf. *Cor.* 2. 1. 92 'a necessary bencher in the Capitol'); 1. 2. 314

Bide upon, dwell upon, insist upon (a point), lit. take one's stand upon; 1. 2. 242

Blank, the white spot in the centre of the target; 2. 3. 5

Blench, swerve from the straight path (of fact or of morality), lit. shy like a horse; 1. 2. 333

Block, (a) blockhead (cf. *Jul. Caes.* 1. 1. 40 'you blocks, you stones'), (b) wooden mould for a hat, or the hat itself; 1. 2. 225

Boiled-brains, i.e. hot-headed youths; 3. 3. 63

Bolted, sifted. A 'bolt' or 'bolter' = a sieve, a strainer; 4. 4. 361

Boor, husbandman, peasant; 5. 2. 155

Boot, (i) 'Grace to boot!' = Heaven help me! (cf. 'Saint George to boot' *Ric. III*, 5. 3. 301); 1. 2. 80; (ii) recompense, award; 4. 4. 632

Bourn, boundary; 1. 2. 134

Break-neck, downfall, destruction; 1. 2. 363

Break up, i.e. open (of a letter; cf. *L.L.L.* 4. 1. 56); 3. 2. 131

Bring, i.e. bring forth; 2. 1. 148

Budget, leather wallet or pouch; 4. 3. 20

Bug, bogey, bugbear; 3. 2. 92

Bugle, black bead of glass, cylindrical in shape so as to be threaded on to a dress or in the form of bracelets; 4. 4. 222

Burthen, refrain in a song; 4. 4. 194

Cabin, berth (*N.E.D.* quotes Capt. Smith, 1626, 'a hanging cabben, a Hamacke'); 3, 3. 24

Caddiss, lit. worsted yarn, here used as short for 'caddis ribbon' = a worsted tape, from which garters, etc. were made. *N.E.D.* quotes *Euphues* (Bond, ii. 9) 'the country dame girdeth hir selfe ...straight in the wast with a course caddis.' Caddis garters were also called 'crewel garters' (cf. *Lear* 2. 4. 7); 4. 4. 207

Callet, a scold; 2. 3. 91

Capable, i.e. of learning or understanding (cf. *All's Well*, G. and *L.L.L.* 4. 2. 82); 4. 4. 759

Caparison, lit. the elaborately ornamented trappings of a horse, hence—outfit; 4. 3. 27

Carbonadoed, cut up or slashed for broiling; 4. 4. 262

Career, the gallop or charge in a tournament or the manage; 1. 2. 286

Carriage, execution, conduct; 3. 1. 17

Case, (a) skin, (b) condition; 4. 4. 805

Censure, opinion, judgment; 2. 1. 37

Centre, lit. the centre of the earth (which in the Ptolemaic astronomy was the centre of the universe), and so fig. man's soul (cf. *Son.* 146 'Poor soul, the centre of my sinful earth,' and *Ham.* 2. 2. 159); 1. 2. 138; 2. 1. 102

Charge, lit. load, weight, hence—importance, value; 4. 4. 255

Chase (sb.), hunted animal, quarry (cf. *N.E.D.* 4 and Turbervile, *Booke of Hunting*, p. 7 'And kill at force, hart, hind, buck, doe... and every chace'); 3. 3. 57

Chase (vb.), harass (with a quibble upon the military sense); 5. 1. 217

CHEAT, (i) something stolen, theft, cf. Greene, *Third Part of Conny-catching*, 47 (ed. G. B. Harrison) 'A cunning villaine... had long time haunted this Cittizens house, and gotten many a cheat which he carried awaye safely'; 4. 3. 28, (ii) a thievish trick; 4. 3. 118

CHILDNESS, childishness (*N.E.D.* gives no other example before 1856); 1. 2. 170

CHOUGH, jackdaw; 4. 4. 612

CIRCUMSTANCE (out of), without ceremony; 5. 1. 90

CLAMMER, or Clamber. A technical term of bell-ringing; lit = to increase the strokes of the clapper preparatory to stopping altogether, hence—to stop from noise, to silence. Warburton perceived this meaning, was laughed at for his pains, but has been justified by *N.E.D.* (v. 'clamour'); 4. 4. 246

CLAP, strike hands in token of a bargain (cf. *Hen. V*, 5. 2. 134 'and so clap hands, and a bargain'); 1. 2. 104

CLEAR (vb.), purify, acquit, free from guilt (cf. *Lucr.* 354 'The blackest sin is cleared with absolution'); 1. 2. 74; 3. 2. 4.

CLEAR (adj.), serene, innocent; 1. 2. 343

CLIMATE (vb.), reside (from sb. 'climate,' = region, country, without reference to climatic conditions); 5. 1. 170

CLIPPING, embracing; 5. 2. 52

CLOG, encumbrance (cf. *All's Well*, 2. 5. 55); 4. 4. 674

CLOSE, secret; 3. 3. 118

CLOUD, sully, defame; 1. 2. 280

COLLOP, lit. = a cut off a joint of meat, hence—a chip of the old block; 1. 2. 137

COLOUR, pretext; 4. 4. 552

COLOURING, (a) dyeing, (b) giving a specious appearance; 2. 2. 20

COME HOME. Naut. 'home' = towards the ship, hence—'come home' = (of an anchor) away from its hold, so as to drag, v. *N.E.D.* 'home' adv.; 1. 2. 214

COMFORTING. In legal sense = abetting, countenancing (Charlton); 2. 3. 56

COMMEND, entrust, commit; 2. 3. 182

COMMISSION, direction from authority to act in a certain way; 1. 2. 40

COMMODITY, advantage, profit; lit. article for sale; 3. 2. 93

COMPASS, get possession of; 4. 3. 93

CONCEIT, (i) faculty of understanding; 1. 2. 224; (ii) notion, thought; 3. 2. 143

CONCEIVE, un lerst n l; 2. 3. 13

CONCERN, engage the attention of, affect with consideration, care or solicitude, cause trouble; 3. 2. 86

CONDITION, nature, quality; 4. 4. 713

CONDUIT, fountain (in the form of a statue); 5. 2. 53–4

CONSIDER, remunerate, 'tip'; 4. 2. 17; 4. 4. 789

COPE WITH, have to do with; 4. 4. 421

CORDIAL, restorative, reviving; 5. 3. 77

COUNTERS, token coins used for arithmetical calculations; 4. 3. 36

COZENER, cheat, impostor; 4. 4. 251

CRACK, flaw, defect; 1. 2. 322

CRONE, withered old woman; 2. 3. 77

CROWN IMPERIAL, the cultivated fritillary (*Fritillaria Imperialis*); 4. 4. 126

CURIOUS, requiring care and attention; 4. 4. 511

CURST, savage; 3. 3. 124

CUSTOM, trade; 5. 2. 97

CYPRESS, crape, black lawn; 4. 4. 219

DEAD, mortal, deadly (cf. *M.N.D.* 3. 2. 57); 4. 4. 431

DELIVERED, (*a*) delivered (as goods), (*b*) declared; 4. 4. 357

DEUCALION, the Noah of classical mythology; 4. 4. 428

DIBBLE, instrument for making holes in the ground for planting seeds, etc.; 4. 4. 100

DILDO, lit. the phallus. The word is often found in ballad refrains; 4. 4. 194

DIS, Pluto; 4. 4. 118

DISCASE, undress (cf. *Temp.* 5. 1. 85 'I will discase me'); 4. 4. 629

DISCHARGED, got rid of, over and done with; 2. 3. 11

DISCONTENTING, displeased; 4. 4. 529

DISCOVER, divulge, reveal; 2. 1. 50

DISCOVERY, disclosure; 1. 2. 441

DISLIKEN, disguise; 4. 4. 647

DISPUTE, discuss, reason about; 4. 4. 397

DOXY, cant term for a beggar's mistress; 4. 3. 2

DRAB, harlot; 4. 3. 27

EARNEST, money paid as an instalment; 4. 4. 640

ENCOUNTER, external behaviour (cf. *Ham.* 5. 2. 199 'outward habit of encounter'); 3. 2. 49

EXCREMENT, anything that grows from the body, e.g. hair, nails, etc.; 4. 4. 708–9

EXERCISE, (*a*) religious observance, (*b*) recreation; 3. 2. 240

EXERCISES, athletics, field sports, military exercises (cf. *A.Y.L.* 1. 1. 67); 4. 2. 32

EXTEMPORE, without taking thought or trouble; 4. 4. 672

EXTREME, hyperbole; 4. 4. 6

EYE-GLASS, the crystalline lens of the eye; 1. 2. 268

FACT, crime; 3. 2. 85

FADING, 'with a fading' = the refrain of a popular song of an indecent character (*N.E.D.*); 4. 4. 195

FAIL, failure; 2. 3. 170; 5. 1. 27

FANCY, love; 4. 4. 479

FARDEL, bundle; 4. 4. 713

FARRE, old comp. of 'far'; 4. 4. 428

FASHION, 'of all fashion' = of all sorts (cf. *Per.* 4. 2. 84 'gentlemen of all fashions'); 3. 2. 104

FAVOUR, countenance, face; 5. 2. 47

FEATLY, gracefully; 4. 4. 176

FEDARY, accomplice; 2. 1. 90

FEEDING, lit. feeding-ground for sheep, landed property; 4. 4. 169

FEELING, heartfelt; 4. 2. 7

FETCH OFF, do for, overcome, kill; 1. 2. 334

FIXURE, stability; 5. 3. 67

FLAP-DRAGON (vb.), swallow down an object. 'Flap-dragon' was a 'play in which they catch raisins out of burning brandy and, extinguishing them by closing the mouth, eat them' (Johnson); cf. the mod. 'snap-dragon' at Christmas; 3. 3. 95

FLATNESS, completeness (cf. *L.L.L.* 3. 1. 100 'that's flat'); 3. 2. 122

FLAUNTS, ostentatious finery; 4. 4. 23

FLAX-WENCH, female flax-worker (as a type of coarse woman); 1. 2. 277

FLAYED, skinned; 4. 4. 636

FLOWER-DE-LUCE, iris; 4. 4. 127

FOOTING, (a) foothold, (b) establishment, endowment; 3. 3. 106

FOOTMAN, foot soldier; 4. 3. 63

FORCED, far-fetched, strained; 4. 4. 41

FRANKLIN, yeoman; 5. 2. 155

FREE, (i) generous; 2. 2. 44; (ii) innocent (cf. *Ham.* 2. 2. 590 'Make mad the guilty and appal the free'); 2. 3. 30; (iii) gracious, willing; 4. 4. 545

FRIENDSHIP, favour, friendly aid (cf. *M.V.* 1. 3. 165); 4. 2. 19

FRONT, (a) forehead, (b) opening period (cf. *Son.* 102 'Philomel in summer's front doth sing'); 4. 4. 3.

GALLIMAUFRY, jumble, hotchpotch, lit. a dish of hashed odds and ends; 4. 4. 325–6

GAP (v. note); 4. 4. 197

GENERATION, offspring (cf. 'generation of vipers'); 2. 1. 148

GEST, lit. a stage of a royal progress or journey, hence—the time allotted for such a stage or halt; 1. 2. 41

GILLYVOR, clove-scented pink; 4. 4. 82

GIVE, consider, set down as; 3. 2. 95

GLASS, i.e. hour-glass; 1. 2. 306

GLIB, geld, castrate; 2. 1. 149

GO ABOUT TO, intend to; 4. 4. 217

GOOD DEED (adv.), indeed, in sooth; 1. 2. 42

GOSSIP, godparent; 2. 3. 41

GRACE, reputation, credit; 2. 1. 122

GRACE TO BOOT! v. *boot*; 1. 2. 80

GUILTY TO, to blame for (cf. *Err.* 3. 2. 162 'guilty to self-wrong'); 4. 4. 535

GUST, taste, catch the flavour of, perceive (cf. *relish*); 1. 2. 219

HAMMER OF (vb.), deliberate earnestly, turn a plan over in one's mind; 2. 2. 49

HAND, deal with, handle; 4. 4. 345

HAND-FAST (in), under arrest; 4. 4. 763

HANDS, 'to be a man of one's hands' = to be a man of vigour and courage; 5. 2. 162

HAPPY MAN BE HIS DOLE! Proverbial = may his dole (i.e. lot) be that of a happy man; 1. 2. 163

HARLOT, lewd; 2. 3. 4.

HAVING, property, wealth; 4. 4. 714

HEAT. *N.E.D.* suggests doubtfully 'to run swiftly over, as in a race'; 1. 2. 96

HEFT, heaving, retching (of one who vomits); 2. 1. 45

HENT, seize, perhaps in the sense of 'take' (= vault); 4. 3. 122

HISTORY, story of any kind, often (as here) = dramatic story, tragedy; 3. 2. 36

HOMELY, rude, uncomely; 4. 4. 330, 423

HONEST, chaste; 2. 3. 71

HONESTY, chastity; 1. 2. 288; 2. 1. 155

HORNPIPE, a wind instrument, said to have been so called from having the bell and mouthpiece made of horn (*N.E.D.*); 4. 3. 44

HORSE (vb.), set one thing upon another, suggesting a jogging motion and perhaps also the sense of 'covering' (the mare by the stallion)—a common meaning of 'horse' (v. *N.E.D.*); 1. 2. 288

HORSEMAN, mounted soldier; 4. 3. 63

HOX, hamstring; 1. 2. 244

I'FECKS, in faith. *N.E.D.* gives 'fegs, feckins, feggings, fac, feck, fags, faiks, fecks' as distortions of 'fay' or 'faith' with the suffix '-kins, frequent in such trivial quasi-oaths; cf. bodykins, by'r lakin'; 1. 2. 120

IMMODEST, excessive, immoderate; 3. 2. 102

IMPORTANCE, import; 5. 2. 17

IMPOSITION. *N.E.D.* explains 'imputation, accusation, charge,' but quotes no parallel. The word implies the infliction or laying on of a burden (here the hereditary burden of original sin); in connexion with 'two lads' there is also perhaps a glance at the school-slang meaning of 'imposition,' though *N.E.D.* gives no example of this before 1746; 1. 2. 74

INCIDENCY, incident, incidental occurrence; 1. 2. 403

INFLUENCE. Astrol. 'the supposed flowing or streaming from the stars or heavens of an etherial fluid acting upon the character and destiny of men, and affecting sublunary things generally' (*N.E.D.*); 1. 2. 426

INKLE, a kind of linen tape; 4. 4. 207

INSINUATE, wheedle, win by covert means; 4. 4. 729–30

INTELLIGENCING, playing the spy, acting the go-between; 2. 3. 69

ISSUE, (*a*) outcome, (*b*) exit; 1. 2. 188

JAR, tick of the clock; 1. 2. 43

JAY. In reference to women of light character (cf. *M.W.W.* 3. 3. 39; *Cymb.* 3. 4. 51); 4. 3. 10

KILL-HOLE, or kiln-hole, a small building or hovel containing a furnace for drying grain, etc., or for making malt—a convenient place for a quiet chat; 4. 4. 244

KNACK, (i) trifle, trinket; 4. 4. 346; (ii) deceitful or crafty contrivance; 4. 4. 425

LAM-DAMN, thrash to death (v. note); 2. 1. 143

LAND-SERVICE, (*a*) military service, (*b*) 'service' = meal; 3. 3. 92

LAY IT ON, do it in good style, pile it on; 4. 3. 40

LET, permit to remain, leave behind; 1. 2. 41

LEVEL, (i) the aim of someone shooting; 2. 3. 6; (ii) 'in the level of' = within the range of; 3. 2. 81

LIMBER, limp, flabby (v. note); 1. 2. 47

LIMIT, allotted time, prescribed period. Apparently used by Sh. alone in this sense (cf. *Meas.* 3. 1. 214 'Between which time of the contract and limit of the solemnity'; *Ric. III*, 3. 3. 8 'The limit of your lives is out'; *Cor.* 2. 3. 146 'You have stood your limitation'); 3. 2. 106

LIVING, property, landed estate; 4. 3. 95

LOSS, perdition, destruction; 2. 3. 192

LOUD, windy, stormy; 3. 3. 11

LOZEL, or losel, good-for-nothing; 2. 3. 109

LUNES, tantrums, fits of lunacy (cf. *M.W.W.* 4. 2. 20, note; *Troil.* 2. 3. 139); 2. 2. 30

MACE, a spice consisting of the dried outer covering of the nutmeg (*N.E.D.*); 4. 3. 45

MADE UP, complete; 2. 1. 179

MANKIND (adj.), infuriated, mad. Prob. of different orig. from 'mankind' (sb.) though the two forms are confused in usage (v. *N.E.D.*); 2. 3. 68

MANNER or mainour, 'to be taken with the manner' = to be found with stolen goods upon one, hence—to be taken in the act. Manner = a term of A.F. law ('manœuvre' lit. handwork, and so—the article stolen); 4. 4. 723

MARK, a conspicuous object set up to direct men's steps; 4. 4. 8

MART (vb.), traffic; 4. 4. 349

MATERIAL, important; 1. 2. 216

MEAN, tenor (cf. *Two Gent.* 1. 2. 95); 4. 3. 43

MEASURE, stately walk, lit. solemn dance; 4. 4. 727

MEDAL, a metal disk bearing a figure or an inscription, used as a charm or trinket (*N.E.D.*); 1. 2. 307

MEDDLER, one who concerns himself with anything; 4. 4. 320

MEDICINE, physician (cf. *All's Well*, 2. 1. 72; *Macb.* 5. 2. 27); 4. 4. 584

MESS, (i) lit. one of the groups of persons, normally four (sitting together and helped from the same dishes). into which the company at a banquet was commonly divided; 1. 2. 227; (ii) course (of a feast); 4. 4. 11

MILLINER, haberdasher; 4. 4. 192

MISSINGLY, with a sense of loss, with distress; 4. 2. 31

MO, more (in number). Formerly 'more' = more (in quantity) only; 1. 2. 8; 4. 4. 270

MOIETY, half; 4. 4. 803

MORT O' TH' DEER, the note sounded on a huntsman's horn at the death of the deer; 1. 2. 118

MOTION, puppet-show; 4. 3. 93

NAYWARD, denial; 2. 1. 64

NEB, beak; 1. 2. 183

NEXT, nearest; 3. 3. 118, 120

NOTE (out of my), not in my list; 4. 3. 46

OCCASION, opportunity; 4. 4. 823

OFFICE, 'stand officed' = hold office, perform a function in a royal household (cf. *All's Well*, 3. 2. 125 and *Cor.* 5. 2. 68 for 'office' (vb.) in two different senses); 1. 2. 172

OVERTURE, discovery, disclosure; 2. 1. 172

O'ERWEEN, to be arrogant or presumptuous; 4. 2. 8

OWE, own; 3. 2. 38

PANTLER, servant in charge of the pantry; 4. 4. 56

PARCEL, item, small quantity; 4. 4. 255

PART, office, duty, function; 1. 2. 400

PARTLET (Dame); used as the proper name of the hen in *Reynard the Fox*; 2. 3. 76

PASH, dial. word for 'head'. Possibly associated by Sh. with a head of cattle; 1. 2. 128

PASSAGE. course, procedure; 3. 2. 90

PAY HOME, fully repay; 5. 3. 4

PENNYWORTH, bargain; 4. 4. 631

PERFECT, certain, assured (cf. *Cymb.* 3. 1. 73); 3. 3. 1

PERFORMED, completed; 5. 2. 94

PETTITOES, trotters; 4. 4. 603

PIECE, work of art; 5. 1. 94; 5. 3. 38

PIECE UP, make up; 5. 3. 56

PIN AND WEB, name for a disease of the eye, probably characterised by a spot or excrescence like a pin's head, and a film covering the general surface; 1. 2. 291

PINCHED, tormented, on the rack; 2. 1. 51

PLACE, official position (esp. of a minister of state); 1. 2. 448

PLACKET, lit. petticoat, often used in an indelicate sense (cf. *N.E.D.* 3 b); 4. 4. 242

POINT (vb.), show, 'point forth' = indicate; 4. 4. 558

POKING-STICK, or putting-stick, made of iron, steel or brass, and heated in the fire, for adjusting the plaits of starched ruffs; 4. 4. 226

POMANDER, scent-ball hung about the neck; 4. 4. 595

PONDEROUS, weighty, important; 4. 4. 521

POST. Public notices in Sh.'s day were commonly exhibited upon posts; 3. 2. 101

PRACTICE, plot, treason (cf. *Tw. Nt.* 5. 1. 363); 3. 2. 166

PRANK UP, dress up in a showy manner; 4. 4. 10

PREDOMINANT. Astrol. in the ascendant, when the 'influence' (q.v.) of the star or planet was at its greatest (v. *All's Well*, G.); 1. 2. 202

PRESENT, immediate; 1. 2. 281; 3. 3. 4

PRESENTLY, at once; 2. 2. 47

PRETENCE, design, purpose (cf. *Two Gent.* 3. 1. 47; *Macb.* 2. 3. 137); 3. 2. 18

PRIG, petty thief (rogues' cant); 4. 3. 98

PROCESS-SERVER, officer who served writs or summonses; 4. 3. 92-3

PROFESS, make professions of friendship or love (cf. *Jul. Caes.* 1. 2. 77 'That I profess myself in banqueting to all the rout'); 1. 2. 456

PROFESSOR, one who makes open profession of religion, a godly person; 5. 1. 108

PROGNOSTICATION, weather forecast for the year according to the almanac. 'Almanacs were published in Shakespeare's time under this title: "An Almanack and Prognostication made for the year of our Lord, 1595"' (Malone); 4. 4. 782-3

PROPER, own; 2. 3. 140

PROPERLY, by right; 2. 1. 170

PUBLISH, denounce or proclaim a person publicly as guilty of this or that; 2. 1. 98

PUGGING. Meaning uncertain, prob. thieving or snatching (v. note); 4. 3. 7

PURCHASE, procure; 4. 3. 27; 4. 4. 508

PURGATION, acquittal (a theol. not a legal term; cf. *Ham.* 3. 2. 318; *A.Y.L.* 1. 3. 53; 5. 4. 43); 3. 2. 7

PUSH (vb.), thrust, strike; 3. 2. 2

PUSH (sb.), pressure of events, a critical juncture; 'upon this push' = at this pinch; 5. 3. 129

PUSH ON, press forward, urge on; 2. 1. 179

PUT FORTH (fig. from sprouting of plants), appear, expose oneself; 1. 2. 254

PUTTER-ON, instigator; 2. 1. 141

PUT TO IT, force one to do one's utmost, drive to extremities; 1. 2. 16

QUALIFY, moderate, appease; 2. 1. 113; 4. 4. 529

QUESTION, conversation; 4. 2.
47

QUICK, alive; 4. 4. 132

QUOIF, 'a tight-fitting cap following
the shape of the head, banded in
front with one or two rolls of
coloured or gold tissue, finishing
at the back in a fall that reached
to the shoulders, and worn far
back so as to show off the hair'
(*Sh. Eng.* ii. 97); 4. 4. 224

RACE (of ginger), root; 4. 3. 46

RAISE, arouse; 2. 1. 198

RAISINS O' TH' SUN, sun-dried
grapes; 4. 3. 48

RASH, swift in operation (cf. *2 Hen.
IV*, 4. 4. 48 'Though it doth
work as strong/As aconitum or
rash gun-powder'); 1. 2. 319

REBELLION, (*a*) revulsion of feeling
or desire; cf. *All's Well*, G.,
(*b*) revolt in the political sense;
1. 2. 355

RED, flushed; 4. 4. 54

REHEARSE, tell, narrate; 5. 2. 60

RELATION, narrative; 5. 3. 130

RELISH, lit. taste or have a taste,
hence—(i) perceive; 2. 1. 167,
(ii) prove appetising, be accept-
able; 5. 2. 120

REPLENISHED, complete, perfect
(cf. *Ric. III*, 4. 3. 18 'The most
replenished sweet work of
nature'); 2. 1. 79

REQUIRE, need, demand by right,
deserve; 2. 3. 190; 3. 2. 63

RESPECTING, in comparison with;
5. 1. 35

REVOLTED, unfaithful (cf. *Tw. Nt.*
G.); 1. 2. 199

RHEUM, lit. morbid defluxion of the
humours, rheumatism (cf. *Meas.*
3. 1. 31 'the gout, serpigo, and
the rheum'); 4. 4. 396

RIFT (vb.), split; 5. 1. 66

ROUND (vb.), whisper secretly; 1. 2.
217

ROVER, lit. pirate. Leontes perhaps
means 'scamp'; 1. 2. 176

SAFFRON, orange-red product consisting of the dried stigmas of the
autumnal crocus, used chiefly for
colouring confectionery, liquors,
etc. and for flavouring; formerly
extensively used in medicine as a
cordial and a sudorific (*N.E.D.*);
4. 3. 44

SALTIER, blunder for 'satyr'; 4. 4.
324

SAVORY, a garden herb for flavouring
food, akin to thyme; 4. 4.
104

SCAPE, breach of chastity, cf. Wil-
son, *Rhetorique*, 1553, 'maidens
that have made a scape are
commonly called to be nurses';
3. 3. 71

SCOUR, hurry; 2. 1. 35

SECOND, 'to be second to' = to
lend support to; 2. 3. 27

SEEMING, comeliness; 4. 4. 75

SEIZE, confiscate; 2. 3. 137

SERVICE, v. *land-service*; 3. 3. 92

SESSION, or SESSIONS, a judicial
sitting of a judge or judges to
determine causes, a judicial trial
or investigation (*N.E.D.*); 2. 3.
202; 3. 2. 1

SHE, (i) female, woman; 1. 2. 44;
(ii) mistress, love; 4. 4. 346

SILLY, trifling, petty; 4. 3. 28

SINGULARITIES, rarities; 5. 3. 12

SITTING, interview, reception; 4.
4. 558

SKILL, (i) craft, design; 2. 1. 166;
(ii) ground, course; 4. 4. 152

SLEEVE-HAND, wrist-band, cuff; 4.
4. 209

SLIPPERY, unchaste, licentious; 1.
2. 273

SNEAP, nip or pinch with cold; 1. 2. 13

SOAKING, absorbent, sucking up; 1. 2. 224

SOLELY (adj.), alone; 2. 3. 17

SOME, about, nearly; 2. 1. 145

SPEED, fortune, hap; 3. 2. 144

SPICE, slight taste, a touch, a sample; 3. 2. 183

SPRINGE, trap; 4. 3. 35

SQUARE (sb.), embroidered yoke of a garment; 4. 4. 210

SQUARE (vb.), regulate, frame, direct (by some standard or principle of action); 3. 3. 41; 5. 1. 52

SQUASH, unripe peaspod (applied humorously or in contempt to a person, cf. *Tw. Nt.* 1. 5. 157); 1. 2. 160

SQUIER, foot-rule; 4. 4. 336

STARRED. Astrol. fated; 3. 2. 99

STILL (adj.), continual; 3. 2. 211

STOMACHER, 'ornamental covering for the chest (often covered with jewels) worn by women under the lacing of the bodice' (*N.E.D.*); 4. 4. 224

STRAIN, to violate the spirit of one's oath or the strict requirements of one's conscience (*N.E.D.* 11 b); 3. 2. 50

STRAIT (vb.), put to it, reduce to straits; 4. 4. 351

STRANGE, (*a*) exceptional, (*b*) alien, not of one's kin; 2. 3. 179

STRANGELY, 'as though it were of alien birth' (Moorman); 2. 3. 182

STRIKE. Astrol. blast, destroy by malign influence (cf. *Ham.* 1. 1. 162 'then no planets strike'); 1. 2. 201

STUFFED, full; 2. 1. 185

SUBJECT, i.e. the subjects of a king, the nation as a whole (cf. *Ham.* 1. 1. 72 'nightly toils the subject of the land'); 1. 1. 37

SUDDENLY, at once, very speedily; 2. 3. 200

SUFFICIENCY, ability; 2. 1. 185

TABLE-BOOK or tables, note-book; 4. 4. 595

TAKE, bewitch, charm; 4. 4. 119

TAKE IN, take prisoner, conquer; 4. 4. 574

TAKE UP, (i) cope with, (ii) rebuke; 3. 3. 87

TALL, bold, courageous; 5. 2. 162

TARDY, (vb.) delay; 3. 2. 161

TAWDRY-LACE, a silk 'lace' or neck-tie much worn by women in the 16th and early 17th cents., so called because St Audrey (St Etheldreda) died of a tumour in her throat which she regarded as a just retribution for the vanity of the splendid necklaces worn in her youth. Such tawdry-laces were bought in large numbers at the annual fair of St Etheldreda at Ely; 4. 4. 248

TELL, count; 4. 4. 184

TEMPT, make approaches to, make trial of; 2. 2. 50

THREE-MAN SONG-MEN, i.e. singers of 'three-man-songs' or lively and convivial trios for male voices. *N.E.D.* quotes Heywood, *1st Part Ed. IV*, Works, 1874, i. 51 'Weele have a three-man song, to make our guests merry.' Sometimes called 'free-man's songs'; 4. 3. 41–2

THREE-PILE, 'the most expensive kind of velvet, cut in three heights' (*Sh. Eng.* ii. 102, cf. *Meas.* 1. 2. 33; 4. 3. 9); 4. 3. 14

TIME, 'in good time.' An expression with a variety of meanings, here used indignantly = well, I never! that's good! 4. 4. 163

Toaze, lit. comb out (wool, etc.), hence—elicit by close examination. *N.E.D.* quotes 'toze your conscience' (1633), 'spurious expositions...upon the scriptures in his tedious tozing of them' (1648); 4. 4. 730

Tod (vb.), yield a tod or 28 lbs. of wool; 4. 3. 33

Touch, reach to, attain; 2. 1. 176

Toy, trifle, a thing of no substance; 3. 3. 39

Tremor cordis, palpitation of the heart; 1. 2. 110

Trick, (i) characteristic expression of the face or voice; 2. 3. 101; (ii) puppet, toy, trifle (cf. *Shrew*, 4. 3. 67 'A knack, a toy, a trick, a baby's cap'); 2. 1. 51

Troll-my-dames, or Troll-madam, a game for ladies, something like bagatelle, in which balls were 'trolled' through arches set upon a board; 4. 3. 85

Trumpery, lit. deceitful stuff, hence—rubbish; 4. 4. 594

Trunk-work, 'secret or clandestine actions, as by means of a trunk' (*N.E.D.*). Cf. Iachimo's trunk in *Cymb.*; 3. 3. 73

Tug, contend, strive, cf. *Macb.* 3. 1. 112 'tugg'd with fortune'; 4. 4. 494

Turtle, turtle-dove; 4. 4. 154

Tyrannous, cruel; 2. 3. 28

Tyrant, cruel monster; 2. 3. 116

Unbraided, i.e. new, not shop-soiled. *N.E.D.* gives 'Braided wares: goods that have changed colour, become tarnished, faded'; 4. 4. 203

Uncurrent, out of the ordinary, unfashionable; 3. 2. 49

Undergo, undertake; 2. 3. 164

Unroosted, knocked off one's perch; 2. 3. 75

Unsphere (the stars), remove from their orbits (cf. *M.N.D.* 2. 1. 153–4 'certain stars shot madly from their spheres/To hear the sea-maid's music'). 'A reference to the Ptolemaic system, wherein the moon and the stars were supposed to be fixed in hollow crystalline spheres, which were made to revolve by the highest sphere, the *primum mobile*, and in their revolutions of varying velocity made music' (Furness); 1. 2. 48

Unthrifty to, not eager to increase; 5. 2. 109

Use, profit, advantage; 3. 1. 14

Utter, set in circulation; 4. 4. 321

Vast (sb.), boundless and desolate space (of sea), cf. *Per.* 3. 1. 1 'Thou god of this great vast, rebuke these surges'; 1. 1. 28

Virginalling, touching lightly with the fingers (as if playing upon the virginals). Cf. *Son.* 128 'those jacks that nimble leap To kiss the tender inward of thy hand'; 1. 2. 125

Vulgars, common people; 2. 1. 94

Wag, a merry or mischievous boy; 1. 2. 66

Waggon, chariot; 4. 4. 118

Wakes, 'the local annual festival of an English parish observed (originally on the feast of the patron saint of the church) as an occasion for making holiday, entertainment of friends, and often for village sports, dancing and other amusements' (*N.E.D.*); 4. 3. 99

WARD, attitude taken up by a fencer to protect himself from a blow; 1. 2. 33

WARDEN PIE, i.e. a pie made of Warden pears or apples, so called after the Cistercian Abbey of Warden in Bedfordshire (v. *Sh. Eng.* i. 372); 4. 3. 45

WARP, shrink, change aspect, become distorted; 1. 2. 365

WEAK-HINGED, crazy, rickety (v. note); 2. 3. 119

WEATHER-BITTEN, weather-worn; 5. 2. 53

WEEDS, clothes; 4. 4. 1

WELKIN (adj.), sky-blue; 1. 2. 136

WELL TO LIVE, well-to-do (cf. *M.V.* 2. 2. 49); 3. 3. 115

WHISTLE, talk secretly, whisper (v. *N.E.D.* 10); 4. 4. 244

WILD, headstrong; 2. 1. 182

WIND, one of the four points of the compass (v. note); 1. 1. 29

WINK, sleep; 1. 2. 317

WOE, cry of woe, lamentation; 3. 2. 208

WOMAN-TIRED, henpecked; 2. 3. 75

WORTH, anything that gives value, hence—rank; 5. 1. 214

YEAST, foam or froth; 3. 3. 91

WORDSWORTH CLASSICS

General Editors: Marcus Clapham & Clive Reynard

JANE AUSTEN
Emma
Mansfield Park
Northanger Abbey
Persuasion
Pride and Prejudice
Sense and Sensibility

ARNOLD BENNETT
Anna of the Five Towns

R. D. BLACKMORE
Lorna Doone

ANNE BRONTË
Agnes Grey
The Tenant of Wildfell Hall

CHARLOTTE BRONTË
Jane Eyre
The Professor
Shirley
Villette

EMILY BRONTË
Wuthering Heights

JOHN BUCHAN
Greenmantle
Mr Standfast
The Thirty-Nine Steps

SAMUEL BUTLER
The Way of All Flesh

LEWIS CARROLL
Alice in Wonderland

CERVANTES
Don Quixote

G. K. CHESTERTON
*Father Brown:
Selected Stories*
*The Man who was
Thursday*

ERSKINE CHILDERS
The Riddle of the Sands

JOHN CLELAND
*Memoirs of a Woman of
Pleasure: Fanny Hill*

WILKIE COLLINS
The Moonstone
The Woman in White

JOSEPH CONRAD
Heart of Darkness
Lord Jim
The Secret Agent

J. FENIMORE COOPER
*The Last of the
Mohicans*

STEPHEN CRANE
*The Red Badge of
Courage*

THOMAS DE QUINCEY
*Confessions of an English
Opium Eater*

DANIEL DEFOE
Moll Flanders
Robinson Crusoe

CHARLES DICKENS
Bleak House
David Copperfield
Great Expectations
Hard Times
Little Dorrit
Martin Chuzzlewit
Oliver Twist
Pickwick Papers
A Tale of Two Cities

BENJAMIN DISRAELI
Sybil

THEODOR DOSTOEVSKY
Crime and Punishment

**SIR ARTHUR CONAN
DOYLE**
*The Adventures of
Sherlock Holmes*
*The Case-Book of
Sherlock Holmes*
*The Lost World &
Other Stories*
*The Return of
Sherlock Holmes*
Sir Nigel

GEORGE DU MAURIER
Trilby

ALEXANDRE DUMAS
The Three Musketeers

MARIA EDGEWORTH
Castle Rackrent

GEORGE ELIOT
The Mill on the Floss
Middlemarch
Silas Marner

HENRY FIELDING
Tom Jones

F. SCOTT FITZGERALD
*A Diamond as Big as the
Ritz & Other Stories*
The Great Gatsby
Tender is the Night

GUSTAVE FLAUBERT
Madame Bovary

JOHN GALSWORTHY
In Chancery
The Man of Property
To Let

ELIZABETH GASKELL
Cranford
North and South

KENNETH GRAHAME
*The Wind in the
Willows*

**GEORGE & WEEDON
GROSSMITH**
Diary of a Nobody

RIDER HAGGARD
She

THOMAS HARDY
*Far from the
Madding Crowd*
The Mayor of Casterbridge
*The Return of the
Native*
Tess of the d'Urbervilles
The Trumpet Major
*Under the Greenwood
Tree*

Distribution

AUSTRALIA, BRUNEI
& MALAYSIA
Reed Editions
22 Salmon Street, Port Melbourne
Vic 3207, Australia
Tel: (03) 245 7111
Fax (03) 245 7333

DENMARK
BOG-FAN
St. Kongensgade 61A
1264 København K

BOGPA SIKA
Industrivej 1, 7120 Vejle Ø

FRANCE
Bookking International
60 Rue Saint-André-des-Arts
75006 Paris

GERMANY, AUSTRIA
& SWITZERLAND
Swan Buch-Marketing GmbH
Goldscheuerstrabe 16
D-7640 Kehl Am Rhein, Germany

GREAT BRITAIN & IRELAND
Wordsworth Editions Ltd
Cumberland House, Crib Street,
Ware, Hertfordshire SG12 9ET

Selecta Books
The Selectabook
Distribution Centre
Folly Road, Roundway, Devizes
Wiltshire SN10 2HR

HOLLAND & BELGIUM
Uitgeverlj en Boekhandel
Van Gennep BV, Spuistraat 283
1012 VR Amsterdam, Holland

INDIA
OM Book Service
1690 First Floor
Nai Sarak, Delhi – 110006
Tel: 3279823-3265303 Fax: 3278091

ITALY
Magis Books
Piazza Della Vittoria l/C
42100 Reggio Emilia
Tel: 0522-452303 Fax: 0522-452845

NEW ZEALAND
Whitcoulls Limited
Private Bag 92098, Auckland

NORWAY
Norsk Bokimport AS
Bertrand Narvesensvei 2
Postboks 6219, Etterstad, 0602 Oslo

PORTUGAL
Isabel Leao **Editorial Noticias**
Rua da Cruz da Carreira, 4B
1100 Lisboa
Tel: 01-570051 Fax: 01-3522066

SINGAPORE
Book Station
18 Leo Drive, Singapore
Tel: 4511998 Fax: 4529188

CYPRUS & GREECE
Huckleberry Trading
4 Isabella, Anavargos, Pafos, Cyprus
Tel: 06-231313

SOUTH AFRICA
Struik Book Distributors (Pty) Ltd
Graph Avenue, Montague Gardens,
7441 P O Box 193 Maitland 7405
South Africa
Tel: (021) 551-5900 Fax: (021) 551-1124

SPAIN
Ribera Libros, S.L.
Poligono Martiartu, Calle 1 – no 6
48480 Arrigorriaga, Vizcaya
Tel: 34-4-6713607 (Almacen)
    34-4-4418787 (Libreria)
Fax: 34-4-6713608 (Almacen)
    34-4-4418029 (Libreria)

USA, CANADA & MEXICO
Universal Sales & Marketing
230 Fifth Avenue, Suite 1212
New York, N Y 10001 USA
Tel: 212-481-3500 Fax: 212-481-3534

DIRECT MAIL
Redvers
Redvers House, 13 Fairmile,
Henley-on-Thames, Oxfordshire RG9 2JR
Tel: 0491 572656 Fax: 0491 573590